COMMON CORE
ENGLISH
WORKBOOK

GRADE
3

prepaze

www.prepaze.com

Author: Ace Academic Publishing

Ace Academic Publishing is a leading supplemental educational workbook publisher for grades K-12. At Ace Academic Publishing, we realize the importance of imparting analytical and critical thinking skills during the early ages of childhood and hence our books include materials that require multiple levels of analysis and encourage the students to think outside the box.

The materials for our books are written by award winning teachers with several years of teaching experience. All our books are aligned with the state standards and are widely used by many schools throughout the country.

Prepaze is a sister company of Ace Academic Publishing. Intrigued by the unending possibilities of the internet and its role in education, Prepaze was created to spread the knowledge and learning across all corners of the world through an online platform. We equip ourselves with state-of-the-art technologies so that knowledge reaches the students through the quickest and the most effective channels.

For inquiries and bulk orders, contact Ace Academic Publishing at the following address:

Ace Academic Publishing
3736 Fallon Road #403
Dublin CA 94568

www.aceacademicpublishing.com

Ace Academic Publishing
ACHIEVING EXCELLENCE TOGETHER

ISBN: 978-1-949383-09-6

INTRODUCTION

About the Book

The content of this book includes multiple chapters and units covering all the required common core standards for the grade level. Similar to a standardized exam, you can find questions of all types - multiple choice, fill in the blanks, true or false, match the correct answer and explain your answers. The carefully chosen reading comprehension passages will help students gain key comprehension skills, such as themes, understanding figurative languages, character traits, and contextual vocabulary. The questions also cover writing standards that are not covered by most of the other commonly available workbooks. The exercises help students learn proper language conventions and effectively use resources to research topics for writing essays. The detailed answer explanations help the students make sense of the problems and gain confidence in solving similar problems.

For the Parents

This workbook includes practice questions and tests that cover all the required Common Core Standards for the grade level. The book comprises of multiple tests for each topic so that your child can retake another test on the same topic. The workbook also includes questions for the writing standards and teaches your child to write essays and free responses. The workbook is divided into chapters and units so that you can choose the topics that you want your child to practice. The detailed answer explanations will teach your child the right methods to solve all types of questions, including the free-response questions. After completing the tests on all the chapters, your child can take any common core standardized exam with confidence and can excel in it.

For additional online practice, sign up for a free account at www.aceacademicprep.com.

For the Teachers

All questions and tests included in the workbook are based on the core state standards and include a clear label of the standard name. By following the chapter by chapter units, you can assign your students tests on a particular topic. The workbook will help your students overcome any deficiencies in their understanding of critical concepts and will also help you identify the specific topics that may require more practice. The grade-appropriate, yet challenging questions will help your students learn to strategically use the appropriate tools and persevere through common core standardized exams.

For additional online practice, sign up for a free account at www.aceacademicprep.com.

prepaze

Other books from Ace Academic Publishing

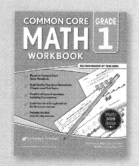

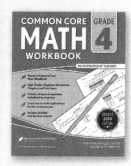

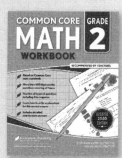
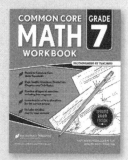
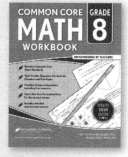

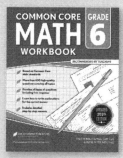

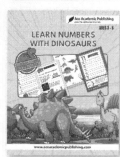

Ace Academic Publishing
ACHIEVING EXCELLENCE TOGETHER

TABLE OF CONTENTS GRADE 3

1. READING: LITERATURE

1. READING: LITERATURE

~ 1.1. Key Ideas and Details ~

Common Core State Standards: CCSS.ELA-LITERACY.RL.3.1, CCSS.ELA-LITERACY.RL.3.2, CCSS.ELA-LITERACY.RL.3.3

Skills:

- Demonstrate an understanding of a text
- Recount stories and determine the central message
- Describe characters in a story

> ➤ **Directions:** *Read the passage and answer the questions below.*

=== **EXAMPLE** ===

Coach Smith was pessimistic about winning another championship. It pained him to imagine breaking the team's six-year winning streak. As he glared at all the trophies on his mantelpiece, he thought about the team's rough journey. There had been many disappointments and losses this particular football season. He recalled the injury that permanently benched his star player. He could still hear the fans booing at the devastating homecoming loss. He sighed in despair as he envisioned the future of the team. He wondered if this was the end of a victorious reign.

E1   Why was Coach Smith pessimistic about winning the championship this year? (RL.3.1)

  A. The team was failing due to losses and an injury.
  B. He did not like football anymore.
  C. The championship game was canceled due to weather.
  D. Someone had stolen his football trophies.

Answer: A. The team was failing due to losses and an injury. The text states that there had been many disappointments and losses, including an injury.

1. READING: LITERATURE

═══ **EXAMPLE** ═══

THE ANT AND THE GRASSHOPPER

In a field one summer's day a Grasshopper was hopping about, chirping and singing to

its heart's content. An Ant passed by, bearing along with great toil an ear of corn he was taking to the nest.

"Why not come and chat with me," said the Grasshopper, "instead of toiling and moiling in that way?"

"I am helping to lay up food for the winter," said the Ant, "and recommend you to do the same."

"Why bother about winter?" said the Grasshopper; we have got

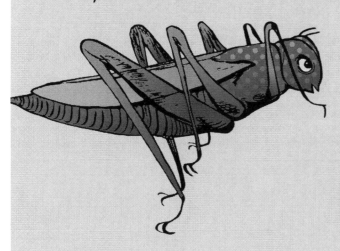

plenty of food at present." But the Ant went on its way and continued its toil. When the winter came the Grasshopper had no food and found itself dying of hunger, while it saw the ants distributing every day corn and grain from the stores they had collected in the summer. Then the Grasshopper knew: It is best to prepare for the days of necessity.

E2 **What is the central message of this story?** (RL.3.2)

A. Ants like to store food for the winter.

B. It is best to prepare for the days of necessity.

C. Grasshoppers are lazy.

D. It is best to distribute corn and grain in the summer.

Answer: **B.** It is best to prepare for the days of necessity. The central message of a story is a lesson or moral that the author wants to convey. In this story, the central message is conveyed through the characters' experiences. The grasshopper learned to always be prepared, which is the central message of this story.

1. READING: LITERATURE

EXAMPLE

Mrs. Griswold was a grumpy old lady. She always scoffed at kids and hissed away cats in the neighborhood. She had a sign on her fence that said: Keep Out. This was fitting for Mrs. Griswold because she wanted to be alone all the time. And in turn, nobody wanted to go anywhere near her. Whenever people saw her, they would quickly run away. This was because Mrs. Griswold was quite scary. *Everyone* in the neighborhood was afraid of her. I wasn't afraid, though. I was brave. That is how the adventure began.

E3 Which word best describes Mrs. Griswold? (RL.3.3)

A. Grumpy **B.** Friendly
C. Interesting **D.** Comical

Answer: **A.** The text describes Mrs. Griswold as grumpy.

1. READING: LITERATURE

> **Directions:** *Read the passage and answer the questions below.*

THE BOX-CAR CHILDREN

Around four o'clock the children took a long walk in the opposite direction from any of their other explorations. They were rewarded by two discoveries. One was a hollow tree literally filled with walnuts, gathered presumably by a thrifty squirrel the previous fall. The other discovery frightened them a little just at first. For with bristling back and a loud bark, Watch suddenly began to rout out something in the leaves, and that something began to cackle and half run and half fly from the intruders. It was a runaway hen. The children succeeded in catching the dog and reducing him to order, although it was clear he liked very much to chase hens.

"She had some eggs, too," remarked Benny as if trying to make pleasant conversation.

Jess bent over incredulously and saw a rude nest in the moss in which there were five eggs.

"A runaway hen!" said Henry, hardly believing his eyes. "She wants to hide her nest and raise chickens."

The children had no scruples at all about taking the eggs.

"Almost a gift from heaven," said Violet, stroking one of the eggs with a delicate finger. "It wouldn't be polite to refuse them."

Scrambled eggs made a delicious supper for the children. Jess  broke all the eggs into the biggest bowl and beat them vigorously with a spoon until they were light and foamy. Then she added milk and salt and delegated Violet to beat them some more while she prepared the fire. The big kettle, empty and clean, was hung over the low fire and butter was dropped in. Jess watched it anxiously, tipping the kettle slightly in all directions. When the butter had reached the exact shade of brown, Jess poured in the eggs and stirred them carefully, holding her skirts away from the fire. She was amply repaid for her care when she saw her family attack the meal. Clearly, this was a feast day.

prepaze

1. READING: LITERATURE

=== **MULTIPLE CHOICE** ===

1. **Which sentence best describes what happened during the children's long walk?** (RL.3.1)
   A. Around four o'clock, the children took a long walk in the opposite direction from any of their other explorations.
   B. She was amply repaid for her care when she saw her family attack the meal.
   C. They were rewarded by two discoveries.
   D. "She had some eggs, too," remarked Benny as if trying to make pleasant conversation.

2. **What did the children discover first?** (RL.3.1)
   A. A hollow tree   B. A thrifty squirrel
   C. A runaway hen   D. A dog named Watch

3. **What was the second discovery?** (RL.3.1)
   A. A thrifty squirrel   B. A hollow tree
   C. A runaway dog   D. A runaway hen

4. **How did the children feel about the second discovery at first?** (RL.3.1)
   A. Sad   B. Alarmed   C. Cheerful   D. Annoyed

5. **Which sentence best describes how the children felt about the second discovery?** (RL.3.1)
   A. The other discovery frightened them a little at first.
   B. The children succeeded in catching the dog and reducing him to order, although it was clear he liked very much to chase hens.
   C. Clearly, this was a feast day.
   D. They were rewarded by two discoveries.

6. **Which sentence best describes where the children found the eggs?** (RL.3.1)

A. Jess bent over incredulously and saw a rude nest in the moss in which there were five eggs.

B. "She wants to hide her nest and raise chickens."

C. "Almost a gift from heaven," said Violet, stroking one of the eggs with a delicate finger.

D. Watch suddenly began to rout out something in the leaves.

═══════ **FREE RESPONSE** ═══════

7. **How did the children feel about their decision regarding the eggs? Use textual evidence in your response.** (RL.3.1)

_____

_____

_____

_____

1.1. KEY IDEAS AND DETAILS

> **Directions:** *Read the passage and answer the questions below.*

THE FOX AND THE STORK

The Fox one day thought of a plan to amuse himself at the expense of the Stork, at whose odd appearance he was always laughing.

"You must come and dine with me today," he said to the Stork, smiling to himself at the trick he was going to play. The Stork gladly accepted the invitation and arrived in good time and with a very good appetite.

For dinner the Fox served soup. But it was set out in a very shallow dish, and all the Stork could do was to wet the very tip of his bill. Not a drop of soup could he get. But the Fox lapped it up easily, and, to increase the disappointment of the Stork, made a great show of enjoyment.

...continued next page

1. READING: LITERATURE

The hungry Stork was much displeased at the trick, but he was a calm, even-tempered fellow and saw no good in flying into a rage. Instead, not long afterward, he invited the Fox to dine with him in turn. The Fox arrived promptly at the time that had been set, and the Stork served a fish dinner that had a very appetizing smell. But it was served in a tall jar with a very narrow neck. The Stork could easily get at the food with his long bill, but all the Fox could do was to lick the outside of the jar, and sniff at the delicious odor. And when the Fox lost his temper, the Stork said calmly: Do not play tricks on your neighbors unless you can stand the same treatment yourself.

MULTIPLE CHOICE

1.1. KEY IDEAS AND DETAILS

8. **What was most likely the reason behind the Fox's trick?** (RL.3.2)
   A. The Fox wanted to amuse himself by making fun of the Stork.
   B. The Fox lost his old soup recipe.
   C. The Fox wanted to visit a faraway land.
   D. The Fox was very friendly.

9. **How did the Stork feel about Fox's trick?** (RL.3.2)
   A. Amused   B. Puzzled   C. Unhappy   D. Terrified

10. **Which sentence best describes how Stork felt about Fox's trick?** (RL.3.2)
    A. The Stork could easily get the food with his long bill.
    B. The hungry Stork was much displeased at the trick, but he was a calm, even-tempered fellow and saw no good in flying into a rage.
    C. The Stork gladly accepted the invitation and arrived in good time and with a very good appetite.
    D. "You must come and dine with me today," he said to the Stork.

1. READING: LITERATURE

11. How did the Stork react to Fox's plan? (RL.3.2)

   A. He yelled at the Fox.

   B. He invited the Fox to dinner.

   C. He ate all of Fox's soup.

   D. He became good friends with the Fox.

12. What was most likely the reason behind the Stork's reaction? (RL.3.2)

   A. The Stork thought that the Fox was funny.

   B. The Stork loved Fox's soup.

   C. The Stork wanted to share food with the Fox.

   D. The Stork wanted to play a trick on the Fox.

13. What is the central message of this story? (RL.3.2)

   A. It is best to eat dinner with a friend.

   B. Do not play tricks on others if you do not like to be tricked.

   C. Do not invite others to dinner if you do not like their food.

   D. Soup is best eaten in the winter.

> ➤ **Directions:** *Read the passage and answer the questions below.*

TALE OF JOHNNY TOWN-MOUSE

Sometimes on Saturdays he went to look at the hamper lying by the gate, but he knew better than to get in again. And nobody got out, though Johnny Town-mouse had half promised a visit.

The winter passed; the sun came out again; Timmy Willie sat by his burrow warming his little fur coat and sniffing the smell of violets and spring grass. He had nearly forgotten his visit to town. When up the sandy path all spick and span with a brown leather bag came Johnny Town-mouse!

Timmy Willie received him with open arms. "You have come at the best of all the year, we will have herb pudding and sit in the sun."

"Hmm! It is a little damp," said Johnny Town-mouse, who was carrying his tail under his arm, out of the mud.

... continued next page

Copyrighted Material   **prepaze**

1. READING: LITERATURE

"What is that fearful noise?" he started violently.

"That?" said Timmy Willie, "that is only a cow; I will beg a little milk, they are quite harmless, unless they happen to lie down upon you."

MULTIPLE CHOICE

14. **Which statement best describes the characters in the story?** (RL.3.3)

   A. Timmy Willie is kind to Johnny Town-mouse.
   B. Timmy Willie is afraid of Johnny Town-mouse.
   C. Timmy Willie and Johnny Town-mouse are enemies.
   D. Timmy Willie and Johnny Town-mouse are children.

15. **Which word best describes Timmy Willie?** (RL.3.3)

   A. Unfair   **B.** Lonely   **C.** Polite   **D.** Grouchy

16. **Which sentence from the story best describes Timmy Willy's character?** (RL.3.3)

   A. Timmy Willie sat by his burrow warming his little fur coat..
   B. Timmy Willie received him with open arms.

   C. "That?" said Timmy Willie, "that is only a cow; I will beg a little milk..."

   D. He had nearly forgotten his visit to town.

> **Directions:** *Read the passage and answer the questions below.*

TALE OF JOHNNY TOWN-MOUSE

"Whatever is that fearful racket?" said Johnny Town-mouse.
"That is only the lawn-mower; I will fetch some of the grass clippings presently to make your bed. I am sure you had better settle in the country, Johnny."
"Hmm—we shall see by Tuesday week; the hamper is stopped while they are at the seaside."

...continued next page

1.1. KEY IDEAS AND DETAILS

prepaze

www.prepaze.com

1. READING: LITERATURE

"I am sure you will never want to live in town again," said Timmy Willie.

But he did. He went back in the very next hamper of vegetables; he said it was too quiet!

One place suits one person, another place suits another person. For my part I prefer to live in the country, like Timmy Willie.

=== **MULTIPLE CHOICE** ===

17. Which word best describes Timmy Willie's attitude towards the country setting? (RL.3.3)

- **A.** Timmy does not want to live in the country.
- **B.** Timmy prefers to live in the country.
- **C.** Timmy has never lived in the country.
- **D.** The text does not reveal where Timmy lives.

18. Which sentence best helps to identify Johnny Town-mouse's attitude towards the country setting? (RL.3.3)

- **A.** "I am sure you will never want to live in town again," said Timmy Willie.
- **B.** "I am sure you had better settle in the country, Johnny."
- **C.** One place suits one person, another place suits another person.
- **D.** He went back in the very next hamper of vegetables; he said it was too quiet!

=== **TRUE OR FALSE** ===

19. Johnny most likely did not like the loud noises in the country. (RL.3.3)

A. True   **B.** False

20. Timmy will most likely move to town with Johnny, based on the text. (RL.3.3)

A. True   **B.** False

1.2. CRAFT AND STRUCTURE

1.1. KEY IDEAS AND DETAILS

1. READING: LITERATURE

1.2. Craft and Structure

Common Core State Standard: CCSS.ELA-LITERACY.RL.3.4, CCSS.ELA-LITERACY.RL.3.5, CCSS. ELA-LITERACY.RL.3.6

Skills:

- Determine the meaning of words and phrases
- Refer to parts of a text (chapter, stanza, etc.)
- Distinguish personal point of view from that of the narrator/characters

➢ **Directions:** *Read the passage and answer the questions below.*

EXAMPLE

Jazz music was invented back in the late 1800s. It first became popular in New Orleans, Louisiana. By the 1920s, jazz music had become more **widespread**. People in other cities, such as Chicago and New York, were playing and listening to jazz music. This period of time was known as the Jazz Age. Eventually, jazz music began to evolve and influence other styles of music. This includes funk, rock and roll, and hip-hop music. Today, jazz is a very important part of American music and culture.

E1   What does the word *widespread* mean in the context of this text? (RL.3.4)

A. Spacious   B. Well-known
C. Misunderstood   D. Secretive

Answer: B. The word *widespread* means well-known in the context of this text.

1. READING: LITERATURE

EXAMPLE

Bed in Summer

by Robert Louis Stevenson

1 In winter I get up at night
And dress by yellow candle-light.
In summer, quite the other way,
I have to go to bed by day.

2 I have to go to bed and see
The birds still hopping on the tree,
Or hear the grown-up people's feet
Still going past me in the street.

3 And does it not seem hard to you,
When all the sky is clear and blue,
And I should like so much to play,
To have to go to bed by day?

prepaze

1. READING: LITERATURE

E2 **How many stanzas are in this poem?** (RL.3.5)

A. 5   **B.** 11   **C.** 7   **D.** 3

Answer: **D.** A stanza is a group of lines in a poem. This poem has 3 stanzas.

=== **EXAMPLE** ===

My family loves to go on vacations in the summer. We visit a new place every year. One time, we went to see the Grand Canyon in Arizona. This was my favorite trip. There was lots of amazing scenery and the view was breathtaking. I also enjoyed our vacation in Paris. We saw the Eiffel Tower and I learned how to speak French. This year we are going to Puerto Rico. My mom says that it is very warm there. There are also plenty of beaches and delicious food. I'm really looking forward to this year's summer vacation.

E3 **What is the narrator's point of view in this text?** (RL.3.6)

A. First person   **B.** Second person

C. Third person   **D.** Fourth person

Answer: **A.** In the first person point of view, the narrator tells a story about himself/herself. The narrator in this text speaks from the first person point of view.

➤ **Directions:** *Read the passage and answer the questions below.*

REUSE, REDUCE, RECYCLE

"Reduce, Reuse, Recycle." National Institute of Environmental Health Sciences, U.S. Department of Health and Human Services, kids.niehs.nih.gov/topics/reduce/index.htm.ealth.

Waste, and how we choose to handle it, affects our world's environment—that's YOUR environment. The **environment** is everything around you including the air, water, land, plants, and man-made things. And since by now you probably know that you need a healthy environment for your own health and happiness, you can understand why effective waste management is so important to YOU and everyone else. The waste we create has to be carefully controlled to be sure that it does not harm your environment and your health.

...continued next page

1. READING: LITERATURE

You can help by learning about and practicing the three R's of waste management: Reduce, reuse, and recycle! Practicing all three of these activities every day is not only important for a healthy environment, but it can also be fun too. So **let's take a minute** right now to learn more about waste and waste management, so you can become a key player in making our world a safe and healthy place.

You can practice **reduction** by selecting products that do not have to be added to landfills or the waste stream in general. This is really easy to do. First and foremost, buy and use less! If all the other people on the Earth used as much "stuff" as we do in the United States, there would need to be three to five times more space just to hold and sustain everybody. So buy only what you need and use all of what you buy. Or make sure that when you are through with something, you pass it along to other people who can continue to put it to good use. This is especially important when it comes to things that can be dangerous to our environment, such as paint and chemicals.

You can "**reuse**" materials in their original form instead of throwing them away, or pass those materials on to others who could use them too! Remember, **one man's trash is another man's treasure**!

MULTIPLE CHOICE

---

1. **What does the word *environment* most likely mean?** (RL.3.4)

The **environment** is everything around you including the air, water, land, plants, and man-made things.

A. A type of plastic
B. The way people live
C. A group of objects
D. The things in nature's surroundings

1. READING: LITERATURE

2.   **What does the word *reuse* most likely mean?** (RL.3.4)

You can "**reuse**" materials in their original form instead of throwing them away, or pass those materials on to others who could use them too!

A. To use again
B. To replace
C. To run out of something
D. To throw something away

3.   **What does the word *reduction* most likely mean?** (RL.3.4)

You can practice **reduction** by selecting products that do not have to be added to landfills or the waste stream in general.

A. The act of leaving
B. The act of making something less
C. The act of recycling
D. The act of wasting something

4.   **What does the phrase *let's take a minute* most likely mean?** (RL.3.4)

So **let's take a minute** right now to learn more about waste and waste management, so you can become a key player in making our world a safe and healthy place.

A. Let's steal a minute from someone.
B. Let's take a minute on vacation.
C. Let's allow time for something.
D. Let's subtract time.

5.   **What does the phrase *one man's trash is another man's treasure* most likely mean?** (RL.3.4)

...pass those materials on to others who could use them too! Remember, **one man's trash is another man's treasure**!

A. A man threw someone's treasure in the trash can.
B. Someone else may want something that you don't want.
C. There is a hidden treasure in the trash can.
D. A man took out the trash and found a treasure.

1. READING: LITERATURE

=== **TRUE OR FALSE** ===

6. **The phrase _let's take a minute_ is an idiom.** (RL.3.4)

   A. True   **B.** False

7. **Figurative language explains the literal meaning of a word.** (RL.3.4)

   A. True   **B.** False

> ➤ **Directions:** _Read the poem and answer the questions below._

Laughing Song
by William Blake

When the green woods laugh with the voice of joy,
And the dimpling stream runs laughing by;
When the air does laugh with our merry wit,
And the green hill laughs with the noise of it;

When the meadows laugh with lively green,
And the grasshopper laughs in the merry scene;
When Mary and Susan and Emily
With their sweet round mouths sing 'Ha ha he!'

When the painted birds laugh in the shade,
Where our table with cherries and nuts is spread:
Come live, and be merry, and join with me,
To sing the sweet chorus of 'Ha ha he!'

1.2. CRAFT AND STRUCTURE

1. READING: LITERATURE

=== MULTIPLE CHOICE ===

8. **The poem is divided into sections called:** (RL.3.5)

    A. Lines   **B.** Stanzas   **C.** Chapters   **D.** Scenes

9. **How many stanzas are there in this poem?** (RL.3.5)

    A. 30   **B.** 3
    C. 6   **D.** Poems do not contain stanzas

10. **Which of the following is true?** (RL.3.5)

    A. Each line contains a set of stanzas in this poem.
    B. Each chapter contains a set of lines in this poem.
    C. Each stanza contains a set of lines in this poem.
    D. Each scene contains a set of verses in this poem.

11. **Which of these lines appear in the first stanza of the poem?** (RL.3.5)

    A. Come live, and be merry, and join with me
    B. When Mary and Susan and Emily
    C. When the painted birds laugh in the shade
    D. When the air does laugh with our merry wit

12. **Which of these phrases appear in the final line of the poem?** (RL.3.5)

    A. To sing the sweet chorus of 'Ha ha he!'
    B. When the painted birds laugh in the shade
    C. And the dimpling stream runs laughing by
    D. And the green hill laughs with the noise of it

1.2. CRAFT AND STRUCTURE

1. READING: LITERATURE

=================== **WRITING PROMPT** ===================

13. **Write a short poem with 2 stanzas.** (RL.3.5)

_____

_____

_____

_____

_____

_____

_____

_____

_____

1.2. CRAFT AND STRUCTURE

prepaze

1. READING: LITERATURE

> **Directions:** *Read the passage and answer the questions below.*

All About the Three Little Pigs

Once upon a time there was an old pig with three little pigs, and, as she had not enough to keep them, she sent them out to seek their fortunes. The first that went off met a man with a bundle of straw, and said to him, "Please, man, give me that straw to build me a house," which the man did, and the little pig built a house with it.

Presently a wolf came along and knocked at the door, and said, "Little pig, little pig, let me come in!"

To which the pig answered, "No, no, by the hair on my chinny-chin-chin!"

This made the wolf angry, and he said, "Then I'll huff, and I'll puff, and I'll blow your house in!"

So he huffed, and he puffed, and he blew his house in, and ate up the little pig.

The second little pig met a man who was chopping wood, and said, "Please, man, give me some of that wood to build me a house," which the man did, and the pig built his house with it.

Then along came the wolf, and said: "Little pig, little pig, let me come in!"

"No, no, by the hair on my chinny-chin-chin!"

"Then I'll puff, and I'll huff, and I'll blow your house in!"

So he huffed, and he puffed, and he puffed and he huffed, and at last he blew the house down and then ate up the little pig.

The third little pig met a man with a load of bricks, and said, "Please, man, give me those bricks to build a house with," so the man gave him the bricks, and he built his house with them.

Then the wolf came, as he did to the other little pigs, and said, "Little pig, little pig, let me come in!"

"No, no, by the hair on my chinny-chin-chin!

"Then I'll huff, and I'll puff, and I'll blow your house in." Well, he huffed and he puffed, and he huffed and puffed, and he puffed and huffed; but he could not get the house down.

1. READING: LITERATURE

=== **MULTIPLE CHOICE** ===

14. **What is the narrator's point of view in this story?** (RL.3.6)

A. First person   **B.** Second person
C. Third person   **D.** Fourth person

15. **Which sentence best helps to identify the narrator's point of view?** (RL.3.6)

A. "Please, man, give me some of that wood to build me a house,"

B. "No, no, by the hair on my chinny-chin-chin!"

C. "Then I'll huff, and I'll puff, and I'll blow your house in."

D. Once upon a time there was an old pig with three little pigs, and, as she had not enough to keep them, she sent them out to seek their fortunes.

16. **What does the narrator know about the wolf in the story?** (RL.3.6)

A. The narrator does not mention the wolf.

B. The narrator knows the wolf's first and last name.

C. The narrator knows the wolf's thoughts and feelings.

D. The narrator is the wolf.

17. **Which sentence best helps to identify what the narrator knows about the wolf?** (RL.3.6)

A. Then along came the wolf, and said: "Little pig, little pig, let me come in!"

B. This made the wolf angry, and he said, "Then I'll huff, and I'll puff, and I'll blow your house in!"

C. Presently a wolf came along and knocked at the door, and said, "Little pig, little pig, let me come in!"

D. To which the pig answered, "No, no, by the hair on my chinny-chin-chin!"

1.2. CRAFT AND STRUCTURE

1. READING: LITERATURE

1.2. CRAFT AND STRUCTURE

=== **WRITING PROMPT** ===

18. **Write a paragraph, in first person, about your opinion of the wolf in the story.** (RL.3.6)

_____

_____

_____

_____

_____

_____

_____

_____

=== **TRUE OR FALSE** ===

19. **The story is told from the third person point of view.** (RL.3.6)

    A. True   **B.** False

20. **The wolf is narrating the story.** (RL.3.6)

    A. True   **B.** False

1.3. INTEGRATION OF KNOWLEDGE AND IDEAS

1. READING: LITERATURE

~~ 1.3. Integration of Knowledge and Ideas ~~

Common Core State Standard: CCSS.ELA–LITERACY.RL.3.7, CCSS.ELA–LITERACY.RL.3.9

Skills:

- Explain text illustrations and language
- Compare and contrast two texts written by the same author

═══ **EXAMPLE** ═══

It was a cold, dark night at the campsite. A few sparks from the campfire were the only source of light within miles. Ranger Roy reminded us to hide our snacks just in case of bears. We weren't worried about bears, though. The biggest problem we ever had was mosquitos. We'd never seen a bear at Camp Cooley. I tucked my bag of pretzels inside my backpack anyway. At least the ants couldn't feast on them in there. As I zipped up my sleeping bag, I heard the strangest rumbling noise over by the trees. It couldn't be. We'd *never* seen a bear at Camp Cooley. We won't *ever* see any bears at Camp Cooley. That's impossible, right?

E1 **Which word best describes this story's mood?** (RL.3.7)

A. Gleeful   **B.** Annoying   **C.** Funny   **D.** Suspenseful

Answer: **D.** The story's mood is best described as suspenseful. The author uses language to create a sense of suspense in the story.

═══ **EXAMPLE** ═══

STORY 1

Maria was still in disbelief as she looked through the window. This was the last time she would see her beloved home. As Papa drove away, she continued to gaze at the flower garden in the front yard. She and Abuela had planted those flowers together. Now, they were distant memories as Papa drove even further down the road. Why did they have to move anyway? Why New York City? There were plenty of jobs for Papa in Texas. This was a bad idea. She could just feel it.

1. READING: LITERATURE

STORY 2

Today was the big day. Maria was both nervous and excited about the swim meet. She was nervous because this was her first citywide competition. She was excited because there was a lot of buzz about the possibility of her winning. She looked at Mama and smiled as they walked out to the pool area.

"You are going to win this," said Mama. "I believe in you. You're the best swimmer in New York City."

"I know, Mama, but Tina Thompson is pretty good, too. I only beat her by a fraction last time."

Mama replied, "Don't worry about that. Just get out there and try your best today."

"Thanks, Mama. I will," said Maria as she took a deep breath.

E1   **How are these stories alike?** (RL.3.9)

    A. Both stories are about Papa's new job.

    B. Both stories are about Maria.

    C. Both stories take place in Texas.

    D. Both stories are written in a sad tone.

Answer: **B.** Both stories are about the same character, Maria.

1. READING: LITERATURE

> **Directions:** *Read the passage and answer the questions below.*

THE BOX-CAR CHILDREN

When Jess opened her eyes it must have been about ten o'clock in the morning. She sat up and looked all around her. She could see dimly the opening where they had come into the woods. She looked around to see that her family was still safely by her. Then she looked up at the sky. At first she thought it must still be night, and then she realized that the darkness was caused by an approaching storm.

"Whatever, whatever shall we do now?" demanded Jess of the air.

She got up and looked in every direction for shelter. She even walked quite a little way into the woods, and down a hill. And there she stood, not knowing what to do next.

"I shall have to wake Henry up," she said at last. "Only how I hate to!"

As she spoke she glanced into the forest, and her feet felt as if they were nailed to the ground. She could not stir. Faintly outlined among the trees, Jess saw an old freight or box car. Her first thought was one of fear; her second, hope for shelter. As she thought of shelter, her feet moved, and she stumbled toward it.

It really was a freight car. She felt of it. It stood on rusty broken rails which were nearly covered with dead leaves. Then the thunder cracked overhead. Jess came to her usual senses and started back for Henry, flying like the wind. He was awake, looking anxiously overhead. He had not noticed that Jess was missing.

"Come!" panted Jess. "I've found a place! Hurry! hurry!"

Henry did not stop to ask questions. He picked up Benny, telling Violet to gather up the hay. And then they ran headlong through the thick underbrush in Jess' wake, seeing their way only too well by the sharp flashes of lightning.

"It's beginning to sprinkle!" gasped Henry.

"We'll get there, all right," Jess shouted back. "It's not far. Be all ready to help me open the door when we get there!

1. READING: LITERATURE

MULTIPLE CHOICE

1. **Which word best describes the story's mood?** (RL.3.7)

    A. Goofy   **B.** Frightening   **C.** Peaceful   **D.** Exciting

2. **Which sentence best helps to identify the story's mood?** (RL.3.7)

    A. When Jess opened her eyes it must have been about ten o'clock in the morning.

    B. It really was a freight car.

    C. Her first thought was one of fear; her second, hope for shelter.

    D. Henry did not stop to ask questions.

3. **Which word best describes the freight car?** (RL.3.7)

    A. Rugged   **B.** Shiny   **C.** Special   **D.** Heavy

4. **Which sentence(s) best describes the freight car?** (RL.3.7)

    A. She could see dimly the opening where they had come into the woods.

    B. It stood on rusty broken rails which were nearly covered with dead leaves.

    C. She got up and looked in every direction for shelter.

    D. "It's not far. Be all ready to help me open the door when we get there!"

FREE RESPONSE

5. **Explain how the author uses sensory language to create imagery in this text.** (RL.3.7)

_____

_____

_____

1. READING: LITERATURE

_____

_____

_____

_____

_____

_____

_____

_____

═══ TRUE OR FALSE ═══

6. **The story's mood can be described as eerie.** (RL.3.7)

    A. True   **B.** False

7. **The author most likely wants to create joyful imagery.** (RL.3.7)

    A. True   **B.** False

8. **Jess's mood is best described as curious.** (RL.3.7)

    A. True   **B.** False

9. **The author uses descriptive language in the story.** (RL.3.7)

    A. True   **B.** False

1.3. INTEGRATION OF KNOWLEDGE AND IDEAS

1. READING: LITERATURE

> ➤ **Directions:** *Read the passages and answer the questions below.*

STORY 1
TALE OF BENJAMIN BUNNY

One morning a little rabbit sat on a bank. He pricked his ears and listened to the trit-trot, trit-trot of a pony. A carriage was coming along the road. It was driven by Mr. McGregor, And beside him sat Mrs. McGregor in her best bonnet.

As soon as they had passed, little Benjamin Bunny slid down into the road, and set off—with a hop, skip and a jump—to call upon his family, who lived in the woods at the back of Mr. McGregor's garden.

That wood was full of rabbit holes; and in the neatest sandiest hole of all, cousins—Flopsy, Mopsy, Cottontail and Peter.

Old Mrs. Rabbit earned her living by knitting rabbit-wool mittens. She also sold herbs, and rosemary tea, and lavender.

Little Benjamin did not very much want to see his Aunt. He came round the back of the fir tree, and nearly tumbled upon the top of his cousin Peter.

Peter was sitting by himself. He looked poorly, and was dressed in a red cotton pocket-handkerchief.

"Peter," said little Benjamin, in a whisper "who has got your clothes?"

Peter replied, "The scarecrow in Mr. McGregor's garden," and described how he had been chased about the garden, and had dropped his shoes and coat.

1. READING: LITERATURE

STORY 2
TALE OF THE FLOPSY BUNNIES

When Benjamin Bunny grew up, he had a family of his own. They were called The Flopsy Bunnies. As there was not always quite enough to eat, Benjamin used to borrow cabbages from Flopsy's brother, Peter Rabbit, who kept a nursery garden. Sometimes Peter Rabbit had no cabbages to spare.

When this happened, the Flopsy Bunnies went across the field to a rubbish heap, in the ditch outside Mr. McGregor's garden.

Mr. McGregor's rubbish heap was a mixture. There were jam pots and paper bags, and mountains of chopped grass from the mowing machine (which always tasted oily), and some rotten vegetable and an old boot or two. One day, there were a bunch of overgrown lettuce and flowers.

The Flopsy Bunnies ate lots of lettuce. One after another, they became tired, and lied down in the mown grass.

Benjamin was not as tired as his children. Before going to sleep, he put a paper bag over his head to keep off the flies.

The little Flopsy Bunnies slept delightfully in the warm sun. From the lawn beyond the garden came the distant clacketty sound of the mowing machine. The blue-bottles buzzed about the wall, and a little old mouse picked over the rubbish among the jam pots. She rustled across the paper bag, and awakened Benjamin Bunny.

The mouse apologized, and said that she knew Peter Rabbit. While she and Benjamin were talking, close under the wall, they heard a heavy tread above their head. Suddenly, Mr. McGregor emptied out a sackful of lawn mowings right upon the top of the sleeping Flopsy Bunnies! Benjamin shrank down under his paper bag. The mouse hid in a jam pot.

The little rabbits smiled sweetly in their sleep under the shower of grass.

 prepaze

1. READING: LITERATURE

=== **MULTIPLE CHOICE** ===

10. **What are the character similarities in Story 1 and Story 2?** (RL.3.9)
- **A.** Peter Rabbit and Benjamin Bunny are characters in both stories.
- **B.** Peter Rabbit and Mrs. Rabbit are characters in both stories.
- **C.** There is a scarecrow in both stories.
- **D.** There are no character similarities between the two stories.

11. **Which of these settings appear in both Story 1 and Story 2?** (RL.3.9)
- **A.** Mrs. Rabbit's house
- **B.** Mr. McGregor's garden
- **C.** Benjamin Bunny's rabbit hole
- **D.** Peter Rabbit's garden

12. **Which of these characters does not appear in both stories?** (RL.3.9)
- **A.** Peter Rabbit
- **B.** Benjamin Bunny
- **C.** Mrs. McGregor
- **D.** Mr. McGregor

13. **How is the setting similar in Story 1 and Story 2?** (RL.3.9)
- **A.** Both stories take place on a rainy day.
- **B.** Both stories take place at night.
- **C.** Both stories take place indoors.
- **D.** Both stories take place outdoors.

1. READING: LITERATURE

14. How is the character Benjamin Bunny different in Story 2? (RL.3.9)

A. The character Benjamin does not appear in Story 2.

B. Benjamin is older in Story 2.

C. Benjamin's name has changed in Story 2.

D. There are no character differences between the two stories.

15. What do these stories have in common? (RL.3.9)

A. They are written by the same author.

B. They have some of these same characters.

C. They have similar settings

D. All of the above

=== **TRUE OR FALSE** ===

16. Benjamin Bunny is a main character in both stories. (RL.3.9)

A. True **B.** False

17. There is a conflict (or problem) in both stories. (RL.3.9)

A. True **B.** False

18. The mouse character appears in both stories. (RL.3.9)

A. True **B.** False

19. These stories are written by two different authors. (RL.3.9)

A. True **B.** False

20. Two stories with the same characters can have different plots. (RL.3.9)

A. True **B.** False

1.4. CHAPTER REVIEW ▷▷▷

1.3. INTEGRATION OF KNOWLEDGE AND IDEAS

1. READING: LITERATURE

1.4. Chapter Review

> **Directions:** *Read the passage and answer the questions below.*

EYES IN THE SKY

Yesterday, my class went on a field trip to the Johnson Space Center. The Johnson Space Center is a historic landmark located in Houston, Texas. Many people go there to learn more about astronauts and how they explore into outer space. As we entered the building, we were amazed by all of the spacecraft and huge machinery.

First, we visited Rocket Park. We saw an enormous rocket called Saturn V. It was 363 feet tall! We learned that Saturn V was once used to send astronauts to the Moon. Although the Earth's Moon is not habitable, people often visit for research purposes. As I gazed at this stunning rocket, I wondered what it was like to land on the moon.

We also got a chance to see the Apollo Mission Control Center. This is another important part of space history. In 1969, astronauts made their first successful mission to the moon. This flight was known as Apollo 11. The space team back at the Apollo Mission Control Center monitored the flight from special computers. We were shocked to see all the buttons, lights and huge screens!

Finally, the tour was over. As we boarded the bus to return back to school, I pretended to be an astronaut. I wished that the bus was a rocket like Saturn V. I imagined that I was on a mission like Apollo 11. I know that one day I'll go back to the Johnson Space Center. Maybe next time I'll be a real astronaut, not just a student.

1. READING: LITERATURE

═══ **MULTIPLE CHOICE** ═══

1. **What does the word *historic* most likely mean?** (RL.3.4)

   The Johnson Space Center is a **historic** landmark located in Houston, Texas.

   A. Forgotten **B.** Famous **C.** Hidden **D.** Ordinary

2. **What does the word *machinery* most likely mean?** (RL.3.4)

   As we entered the building, we were amazed by all of the spacecraft and huge **machinery.**

   A. Message **B.** Decoration **C.** Equipment **D.** Plan

3. **What does the word *monitored* most likely mean?** (RL.3.4)

   The space team back at the Apollo Mission Control Center **monitored** the flight from special computers.

   A. Crashed **B.** Watched **C.** Ignored **D.** Planned

4. **What does the word *habitable* most likely mean?** (RL.3.4)

   Although the Earth's Moon is not **habitable,** people often visit for research purposes.

   A. Flexible **B.** Naughty **C.** Expensive **D.** Livable

> **Directions:** *Read the passage and answer the questions below.*

MY FATHER'S DRAGON

"One day about four months before I arrived on Wild Island a baby dragon fell from a low-flying cloud onto the bank of the river. He was too young to fly very well, and besides, he had bruised one wing quite badly, so he couldn't get back to his cloud. The animals found him soon afterwards and everybody said, 'Why, this is just exactly what we've needed all these years!' They tied a big rope around his neck and waited for the wing to get well. This was going to end all their crossing-the-river troubles."

...continued next page

Copyrighted Material **prepaze**

1. READING: LITERATURE

"I've never seen a dragon," said my father. "Did you see him? How big is he?"

"Oh, yes, indeed I saw the dragon. In fact, we became great friends," said the cat. "I used to hide in the bushes and talk to him when nobody was around. He's not a very big dragon, about the size of a large black bear, although I imagine he's grown quite a bit since I left. He's got a long tail and yellow and blue stripes. His horn and eyes and the bottoms of his feet are bright red, and he has gold-colored wings."

MULTIPLE CHOICE

5. Why couldn't the dragon go back to his cloud? (RL.3.1)

    A. He was too young to fly.
    B. He had a bruised wing.
    C. He had a rope tied around his neck.
    D. All of the above

6. Why did the other animals want to keep the dragon? (RL.3.1)

    A. They wanted to keep him as a pet.
    B. They wanted to use him to cross the river.
    C. They wanted to use him to make fire.
    D. They did not want to keep the dragon.

7. How did the cat feel about the dragon? (RL.3.1)

    A. The cat wants the dragon to go back to his cloud.
    B. The cat is very afraid of the dragon.
    C. The cat thinks of the dragon as a friend.
    D. The cat has never met the dragon.

8. How does the text describe the dragon's size? (RL.3.1)

    A. He was as big as a black bear.
    B. He was as small as a black cat.
    C. He was tall enough to reach the clouds.
    D. He was longer than the river.

1.4. CHAPTER REVIEW

prepaze   Copyrighted Material   **www.prepaze.com**

1. READING: LITERATURE

> **Directions:** *Read the passage and answer the questions below.*

MY FATHER'S DRAGON

The river was very wide and muddy, and the jungle was very gloomy and dense. The trees grew close to each other, and what room there was between them was taken up by great high ferns with sticky leaves. My father hated to leave the beach, but he decided to start along the river bank where at least the jungle wasn't quite so thick. He ate three tangerines, making sure to keep all the peels this time, and put on his rubber boots.

My father tried to follow the river bank but it was very swampy, and as he went farther the swamp became deeper. When it was almost as deep as his boot tops he got stuck in the oozy, mucky mud. My father tugged and tugged, and nearly pulled his boots right off. At last, he managed to wade to a drier place. Here the jungle was so thick that he could hardly see where the river was. He unpacked his compass and figured out the direction he should walk in order to stay near the river. But he didn't know that the river made a very sharp curve away from him just a little way beyond. So as he walked straight ahead, he was getting farther and farther away from the river.

1.4. CHAPTER REVIEW

═══════ **MULTIPLE CHOICE** ═══════

9. Which of these words best describe the narrator's father? (RL.3.3)

A. Frustrated   **B.** Hopeless   **C.** Persistent   **D.** Lazy

     prepaze

1. READING: LITERATURE

1.4. CHAPTER REVIEW

10. Which details from the text provide the best description of the narrator's father? (RL.3.3)

    A. He ate three tangerines, making sure to keep all the peels this time...

    B. So as he walked straight ahead, he was getting farther and farther away from the river.

    C. My father tugged and tugged, and nearly pulled his boots right off.

    D. My father tried to follow the river bank but it was very swampy...

11. What made the narrator's father leave the beach? (RL.3.3)

    A. The weather was too hot.
    B. The jungle was too thick.
    C. The river was too deep.
    D. The dragon was near.

> **Directions:** *Read the poem and answer the questions below.*

THE FIELDMOUSE

Where the acorn tumbles down,
Where the ash tree sheds its berry,
With your fur so soft and brown,
With your eye so round and merry,
Scarcely moving the long grass,
Fieldmouse, I can see you pass.

...continued next page

1. READING: LITERATURE

Little thing, in what dark den,
Lie you all the winter sleeping?
Till warm weather comes again,
Then once more I see you peeping
Round about the tall tree roots,
Nibbling at their fallen fruits.

Fieldmouse, fieldmouse, do not go,
Where the farmer stacks his treasure,
Find the nut that falls below,
Eat the acorn at your pleasure,
But you must not steal the grain
He has stacked with so much pain.

Make your hole where mosses spring,
Underneath the tall oak's shadow,
Pretty, quiet harmless thing,
Play about the sunny meadow.
Keep away from corn and house,
None will harm you, little mouse.

1.4. CHAPTER REVIEW

=== **MULTIPLE CHOICE** ===

12. Which word best describes the poem's imagery? (RL.3.7)

A. Natural
B. Technical
C. Cosmic
D. Sloppy

13. How does the author create imagery in the poem? (RL.3.7)

A. The author drew a picture of the fieldmouse.
B. The author uses personification to create imagery.
C. The author uses onomatopoeia to create imagery.
D. The author uses descriptive language to create imagery.

 prepaze

NAME: .... DATE: ....

1. READING: LITERATURE

=== **TRUE OR FALSE** ===

14. **The tone of the poem can be described as blissful and happy.** (RL.3.7)

    A. True   **B.** False

15. **The author uses an angry tone in his writing.** (RL.3.7)

    A. True   **B.** False

> ➤ **Directions:** *Read the passage and answer the questions below.*

EXCERPT FROM THE ARTICLE YOUR EYES

Which part of your body lets you read the back of a cereal box, check out a rainbow, and see a softball heading your way? Which part lets you cry when you're sad and makes tears to protect itself? Which part has muscles that adjust to let you focus on things that are close up or far away? If you guessed the eye, you're right!

Your eyes are at work from the moment you wake up to the moment you close them to go to sleep. They take in tons of information about the world around you — shapes, colors, movements, and more. Then they send the information to your brain for processing so the brain knows what's going on outside of your body.

And how about the last time you felt sad, scared, or upset? Your eyes got a message from your brain to make you cry, and the lacrimal glands made many, many tears.

Your eyes do some great things for you, so take these steps to protect them: Wear eye protection when playing racquetball, hockey, skiing, or other sports that could injure your eyes. Wear sunglasses. Too much light can damage your eyes and cause vision problems later in life. For instance, a lens could get cloudy, causing a cataract. A cataract prevents light from reaching the retina and makes it difficult to see. The eyes you have will be yours forever — treat them right and they'll never be out of sight!

prepaze   **www.prepaze.com**

1. READING: LITERATURE

=== FILL IN THE BLANK ===

16. This article is written in the _____ person point of view. (RL.3.6)

17. The writer most likely has a _____ opinion about the topic. (RL.3.6)

=== WRITING PROMPT ===

18. Write a paragraph, in first person, expressing your own opinion about the topic. (RL.3.6)

_____

_____

_____

_____

_____

_____

1.4. CHAPTER REVIEW

➢ **Directions:** *Read the passage and answer the questions below.*

ANANSI AND THE POT OF BEANS (A WEST AFRICAN FOLKTALE)

One day, Anansi the Spider went to a party at his grandmother's house. He loved to eat his grandmother's cooking. Anansi could hardly wait to taste her yams, potatoes, and rice. But he was especially excited about Grandmother's famous beans. Anansi loved beans.

...continued next page

1. READING: LITERATURE

Anansi walked into his grandmother's house. Everyone was sitting at the table. They were eating rice, yams, potatoes and many other delicious foods. But Anansi noticed that no one was eating beans.

"Grandmother, where are the beans?" asked Anansi.

"The beans are not quite ready," said Grandmother, "We must wait until they finish cooking."

Anansi did not like to wait. He wanted those beans right now. Anansi decided that he would trick his grandmother.

"Yes, I will wait for the beans," he said. "but first I need to wash my hands for dinner." Anansi walked to the kitchen. He saw a big pot of beans boiling on the stove. Anansi took a spoon and tasted the beans. He wanted to eat them all, but he knew that Grandmother would be upset. "I will hide some beans for myself," he said. Anansi took a big spoonful of beans and put them in his hat. Just as he did this, he heard his grandmother calling him. Anansi did not want to get caught. He quickly put the hat, and those beans, back on his head. Anansi walked back to the dinner table.

The beans were very hot. Anansi started to sweat. "Are you okay?" asked his grandmother.

"I am fine." replied Anansi.

Anansi was not fine. The beans were burning his head. "I must leave now," he said.

"No, please eat your dinner," said Grandmother "The beans will be ready soon."

Anansi tried to eat his yams but he could no longer stand the hot beans on his head. He tried to lift up his hat to get some air. The hot beans fell out!

"Thief!" shouted everyone. "Anansi has stolen the beans!"

Anansi took his hat off. He was bald!

And that is why spiders are bald. It is a symbol of Anansi's greed.

MULTIPLE CHOICE

19.   What was Anansi's problem in the story? (RL.3.2)

A. Anansi did not want to go to the feast.

B. Anansi did not want to eat beans.

C. Anansi wanted beans more than anything else.

D. Anansi's father-in-law was very ill.

prepaze

20. **What did Anansi do to try and resolve his problem?** (RL.3.2)

   A. He hid beans under his hat.

   B. He cooked his own beans.

   C. He asked his father-in-law for beans.

   D. He bought some beans from the store.

21. **What was most likely the reason behind Anansi's plan?** (RL.3.2)

   A. Anansi wanted to share beans with his family.

   B. Anansi wanted to sell the beans for money.

   C. Anansi was extremely hungry.

   D. Anansi was greedy and wanted the beans for himself.

22. **What is the central message of this story?** (RL.3.2)

   A. It is not polite to gossip.

   B. Friendship is very important.

   C. There are consequences to dishonesty and greed.

   D. It is important to always follow the rules.

> **Directions:** *Read the song lyrics and answer the questions below.*

STARS AND STRIPES FOREVER

1 Let martial note in triumph float

And liberty extend its mighty hand

A flag appears 'mid thunderous cheers,

The banner of the Western land.

The emblem of the brave and true

Its folds protect no tyrant crew;

The red and white and starry blue

Is freedom's shield and hope.

Other nations may deem their flags the best

And cheer them with fervid elation

...continued next page

1.4. CHAPTER REVIEW

prepaze

1. READING: LITERATURE

But the flag of the North and South and West
Is the flag of flags, the flag of Freedom's nation.

2 Hurrah for the flag of the free!
May it wave as our standard forever,
The gem of the land and the sea,
The banner of the right.
Let despots remember the day
When our fathers with mighty endeavor
Proclaimed as they marched to the fray
That by their might and by their right
It waves forever.

3 Let eagle shriek from lofty peak
The never-ending watchword of our land;
Let summer breeze waft through the trees
The echo of the chorus grand.
Sing out for liberty and light,
Sing out for freedom and the right.
Sing out for Union and its might,
O patriotic sons.
Other nations may deem their flags the best
And cheer them with fervid elation,
But the flag of the North and South and West
Is the flag of flags, the flag of Freedom's nation.

=== **MULTIPLE CHOICE** ===

23. How many verses are there in this song? (RL.3.5)

   A. 3   **B.** 2   **C.** 8   **D.** 4

1. READING: LITERATURE

24. What is the common theme in each verse? (RL.3.5)

    A. Stars   **B.** Stripes   **C.** The flag   **D.** Freedom

=== **TRUE OR FALSE** ===

25. The song is divided into parts called chapters. (RL.3.5)

    A. True   **B.** False

26. Verse 2 is the longest verse. (RL.3.5)

    A. True   **B.** False

> **Directions:** *Read the passages and answer the questions below.*

1.4. CHAPTER REVIEW

STORY 1
THE ELDERBUSH

Hand in hand they went out until they were standing in the beautiful garden of their home. Near the green lawn papa's walking-stick was tied, and for the little ones it seemed to come to life. For as soon as they got on it, the round polished knob was turned into a magnificent horse head. A long black mane fluttered in the breeze, and four slender yet strong legs shot out. The animal was strong and handsome, and away they went at full gallop round the lawn.

"Now we are riding miles off," said the boy. "We are riding away to the castle where we were last year!"

As they rode around the grass, Nanny, kept on crying out, "Now we are in the country! Don't you see the farmhouse over yonder? There is an elder tree standing beside it; and the rooster is scraping away the earth for the hens. Look how he struts! And now we are close to the church. It lies high upon the hill, between the large oak-trees, one of which is half decayed. And now we are by the blacksmith's workshop, where the fire is blazing, and men are banging with their hammers until the sparks fly about. Away! Away to the beautiful country seat!"

As they rode around the grass, Nanny, kept on crying out, "Now we are in the country! Don't you see the farmhouse over yonder? There is an elder tree standing beside it;

...continued next page

1. READING: LITERATURE

and the rooster is scraping away the earth for the hens. Look how he struts! And now we are close to the church. It lies high upon the hill, between the large oak-trees, one of which is half decayed. And now we are by the blacksmith's workshop, where the fire is blazing, and men are banging with their hammers until the sparks fly about. Away! Away to the beautiful country seat!"

And all that Nanny (who sat behind on the stick) spoke of flew by in reality. The boy saw it all, but they were really only going aroundthe grass. Then they played in a side avenue, and marked out a little garden on the earth. They took elder blossoms from their hair, planted them, and they grew just like those the old people planted when they were children. They went hand in hand, as the old people had done when they were children. They did not go to the Round Tower, or to Fredericksburg. No, the little girl wound her arms around the boy, and then they flew far away through all Denmark. And spring came, then summer, autumn, and winter. And a thousand pictures were reflected in the eye and in the heart of the boy. The little girl always sang to him, "This you will never forget."

STORY 2
THE FIR TREE

Out in the woods stood a nice little fir tree. The place he had was a very good one. The sun shone on him and there was plenty of fresh air. Around him grew many large-sized pine trees and firs. But the little fir wanted so very much to be a grown-up tree.

He did not think of the warm sun and the fresh air. He did not care for the little cottage children that ran about in the woods looking for wild-strawberries. The children often came with a whole pitcher full of berries, or a long row of them threaded on a straw. They sat down near the young tree and said, "Oh, how pretty he is! What a nice little fir!" But this was what the tree did not want to hear.

At the end of a year he had grown very much, and after another year he was a bit taller. One can always tell by the sprouts how many years old a fir tree is.

...continued next page

1. READING: LITERATURE

"Oh! If only I was a high tree like the others," he sighed. "Then I should be able to spread out my branches, and look into the whole wide world! Then the birds would build nests among my branches. And when there was a breeze, I could bend just as much as the others!

In winter, when the snow lay glittering on the ground, a hare would often come leaping along. The hare would jump right over the little tree. Oh, that made him so angry! But two winters passed, and in the third, the tree was so large that the hare had to go around it. "To grow and grow, to get older and be tall," thought the tree "that, after all, is the most delightful thing in the world!"

In autumn the woodcutters always came and cut some of the largest trees. This happened every year, but now the young fir tree, had grown to a proper size. He trembled at the sight, for the magnificent great trees fell to the earth with noise and cracking. The branches were chopped off, and the trees looked long and bare.

1.4. CHAPTER REVIEW

1. READING: LITERATURE

=== MULTIPLE CHOICE ===

27. What do these stories have in common? (RL.3.9)

   A. They both have children as main characters.

   B. They both have trees and other elements of nature.

   C. They both having talking animals.

   D. These stories share no common themes or characters.

28. Which of these events happened in both stories? (RL.3.9)
   A. The characters go on an adventure.
   B. The trees are chopped down by woodcutters.
   C. The seasons change in the story.
   D. A stick turns into a horse.

29. How is the setting different in these stories? (RL.3.9)
   A. One takes place in the summer, the other takes place in the winter.
   B. One takes place in the daytime, the other takes place at night.
   C. One takes place in a future setting, the other takes place in the past.
   D. One takes place in the woods, the other takes place in a garden.

30. What is the main difference between the tree in Story 1 and the tree in Story 2? (RL.3.9)

   A. The tree in Story 2 is personified (or acts like a human).

   B. The tree in Story 1 is not visited by people.

   C. The tree in Story 2 is not a main part of the story.

   D. There is no clear difference between the trees in each story.

prepaze   **www.prepaze.com**

2. READING: INFORMATIONAL TEXT

2. READING: INFORMATIONAL TEXT

∿ 2.1. Key Ideas and Details ∿

Common Core State Standard: CCSS.ELA-LITERACY.RI.3.1, CCSS.ELA-LITERACY.RI.3.2, CCSS.ELA-LITERACY.RI.3.3

Skills:

- Demonstrate an understanding of a text
- Answer questions by referring explicitly to the text
- Determine the main idea of a text
- Describe the relationship between ideas or concepts related to time, sequence, and cause/effect

=== EXAMPLE ===

Parents should set limits on their child's screen time. A child should have limited viewing hours on computers, devices, and televisions. Doctors say that screen time should not replace sleep, time with friends, or physical activity.

E1   A child should limit their time viewing what? (RI.3.1)

A. Books

B. Magazines

C. Televisions

D. Newspapers

Answer: **C.** A child should have limited viewing hours on computers, devices, and televisions.

=== EXAMPLE ===

There are several steps you need to take if you go mountain climbing. Following the steps closely will help to keep you safe as you climb up a mountain. First, make sure that you have the proper gear and safety equipment before you begin your climb. Next, make sure that your safety equipment is secure. Check for loose ropes, clamps, etc. Also, stay focused. Avoid any distractions that could cause you to fall. Finally, start climbing!

2.1. KEY IDEAS AND DETAILS

prepaze   Copyrighted Material   **www.prepaze.com**

2. READING: INFORMATIONAL TEXT

E2 **What is the main idea of the text?** (RI.3.2)

    A. You should go mountain climbing.

    B. Mountain climbing is dangerous.

    C. There are several steps you need to take if you go mountain climbing.

    D. Safety equipment can be expensive.

Answer: **C.** The main idea of this text is that there are several steps you need to take if you go mountain climbing.

═══════ **EXAMPLE** ═══════

There are just a few simple steps that you need to follow in order to make sugar cookies. First, preheat the oven to 375 degrees. Next, pour 1 cup of white sugar into the mixing bowl. Then, add two eggs and mix it all together. After you form the dough into small balls, place them on the cookie sheet and bake for 8 minutes. Enjoy!

E3 **What is the first step you need to do when baking cookies?** (RI.3.3)

    A. Add two eggs

    B. Preheat the oven

    C. Mix the ingredients

    D. Pour the sugar into a mixing bowl

Answer: **D.** The text says that the first step is to preheat the oven.

2.1. KEY IDEAS AND DETAILS

2. READING: INFORMATIONAL TEXT

> **Directions:** *Read the text and answer the questions below.*

HARRIET TUBMAN

Harriet Tubman was born in Maryland in the 1820s. Born a slave, she worked on a large plantation in the fields. Slaves did not have equal rights. To escape slavery, she knew she had to travel to the North. Slavery was illegal in the North. In 1849, she left Maryland and went to Philadelphia. Using the North Star as her guide, she traveled by night so she would not be caught leaving the plantation. After walking nearly 90 miles by foot, she finally crossed into the free state of Pennsylvania. She used the Underground Railroad to escape. The Underground Railroad was not a railroad at all. It was a secret path slaves would follow to run away. They would hideout to escape into the free states. By using railway terms, slaves could safely communicate with the people who helped them to escape. They had to be careful and would only travel by night. They would stop at a hiding place during the day and rest. Harriet was a famous "conductor" or guide on the Underground Railroad. She made it her job to rescue her family and others living in slavery. Harriet was able to lead hundreds of slaves to freedom.

=== **MULTIPLE CHOICE** ===

1. Was Maryland a free state or a slave state? (RI.3.1)

   A. Free state

   B. Slave state

   C. Half was a free state and half was a slave state

   D. I can't tell from the text

2.1. KEY IDEAS AND DETAILS

2. READING: INFORMATIONAL TEXT

2. **What did Harriet Tubman do as a slave?** (RI.3.1)

 A. She worked in the house.

 B. She worked on a large plantation in the fields.

 C. She washed clothes.

 D. She was a teacher.

3. **Why did Harriet Tubman want to travel to the North?** (RI.3.1)

 A. Her family lived there.

 B. She wanted to move to the North.

 C. She wanted to escape slavery.

 D. She had a new job.

4. **Why did Harriet Tubman travel by night to Philadelphia?** (RI.3.1)

 A. She could travel easier without being caught.

 B. She could see better.

 C. She had friends who could help her at night.

 D. She could only leave at night.

5. **How many miles did Harriet Tubman travel to Philadelphia?** (RI.3.1)

 A. 50 miles on a railroad   **B.** 50 miles on foot

 C. 90 miles on a railroad   **D.** 90 miles by foot

6. **What was the Underground Railroad?** (RI.3.1)

 A. A railroad

 B. A secret path slaves followed to escape

 C. An underground train

 D. A secret train

7. **How did people communicate along the Underground Railroad?** (RI.3.1)

 A. By using sign language

 B. By using drawings

 C. By using light signals

 D. By using railway terms

2.1. KEY IDEAS AND DETAILS

prepaze

2. READING: INFORMATIONAL TEXT

> **Directions:** *Read the passage and answer the questions below.*

TASTE BUDS

The average adult has between 2,000 to 10,000 taste buds. We grow new taste buds about every ten to fourteen days. Did you know that not all of our taste buds are on our tongue? Taste buds can also be found inside our mouth, in our throats, and on the inside of our cheeks. Our taste buds let us know how something tastes by sending messages to our brains. They tell us if what we eat tastes sour, sweet, bitter,

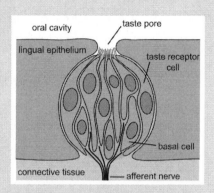

salty, or savory. These different tastes can be felt on all parts of the tongue. The sides of the tongue can detect these tastes the best.

Our sense of taste combines with our sense of smell. This gives food its flavor. When we stick out our tongues in front of a mirror, we can see little pink and white bumps. These are called papillae. Taste buds rest on top of the papillae. When chemicals from food dissolve in saliva, they can be detected by taste buds. This is how we taste our food.

═══ **MULTIPLE CHOICE** ═══

8. **What is the main topic of the text?** (RI.3.2)

    A. Taste buds help us taste our food.

    B. Taste buds are small.

    C. Taste buds detect food chemicals.

    D. We can see pink and white bumps on our tongues.

9. **Our taste buds send messages to our** _____. (RI.3.2)

    A. Stomachs   **B.** Brains   **C.** Noses   **D.** Mouths

10. **What part of the tongue can detect how our food tastes the best?** (RI.3.2)

    A. The middle   **B.** The back   **C.** The front   **D.** The sides

2.1. KEY IDEAS AND DETAILS

2. READING: INFORMATIONAL TEXT

11. Our sense of taste combines with our sense of _____ to give food its flavor. (RI.3.2)

    A. Sight   **B.** Smell   **C.** Touch   **D.** Hearing

12. How do the key details help to develop the main topic of this text? (RI.3.2)

    A. The key details introduce new main topics throughout the text.

    B. The key details explain why some people prefer certain flavors.

    C. The key details further explain how taste buds help us taste our food.

    D. The key details do not help to develop the main topic of this text.

> **Directions:** *Read the passage and answer the questions below.*

HOW TO MAKE A HAWAIIAN PIZZA

A Hawaiian pizza is topped with ham and pineapple pieces. If you want to make a Hawaiian pizza, there are a series of steps that you must follow. You will need pizza dough, a jar of tomato sauce, one cup of mozzarella cheese, one-half cup of ham slices, and one-third cup of pineapple pieces. The first step is to build the layers of your pizza. Start by rolling out the pizza dough with a rolling pin. Secondly, when the dough is flattened, place it on a metal pizza pan. The third step is to evenly spread the tomato sauce on top of the dough. Then, sprinkle the cheese on top of the tomato sauce. Place the ham slices and pineapples on top of the layer of cheese. Now, place the pizza in a 400-degree oven for 10 minutes. The final step is to carefully remove the pizza from the oven, and let it cool. If you try to eat the pizza right away, you might burn your mouth! These seven steps will help you to create a delicious Hawaiian pizza. Enjoy!

2.1. KEY IDEAS AND DETAILS

=== MULTIPLE CHOICE ===

13. If you want to make a Hawaiian pizza, what must you do? (RI.3.3)

    A. You must order a Hawaiian pizza from a restaurant.

    B. You must become a chef.

    C. You must follow a series of steps.

    D. You must own a pizza restaurant.

2. READING: INFORMATIONAL TEXT

14. **How many steps does the text list in order to make a Hawaiian pizza?** (RI.3.3)

A. One   **B.** Three   **C.** Seven   **D.** Five

15. **What is the first step in making a Hawaiian pizza?** (RI.3.3)

A. Build the layers of the pizza   **B.** Clean the oven
C. Flatten the dough   **D.** Grate the cheese

16. **What is the second step in making a Hawaiian pizza?** (RI.3.3)

A. Build your layers   **B.** Flatten the dough
C. Slice the pizza   **D.** Place it in the oven

17. **What is the third step in making a Hawaiian pizza?** (RI.3.3)

A. Buy the ingredients   **B.** Preheat the oven
C. Spread tomato sauce   **D.** Sprinkle the cheese

18. **How long should you bake a Hawaiian pizza?** (RI.3.3)

A. 400 degrees   **B.** 15 minutes   **C.** 30 minutes   **D.** 10 minutes

19. **What should you do after baking the pizza?** (RI.3.3)

A. Preheat the oven
B. Roll the dough
C. Remove the pizza from the oven
D. Eat the pizza

20. **How do these steps work together?** (RI.3.3)

A. Each step leads to the next step in order to create a Hawaiian pizza.
B. The steps can be followed in any order to create of a Hawaiian pizza.
C. The steps help you shop for the ingredients to make a Hawaiian pizza.
D. Each step explains the history of a Hawaiian pizza.

2.2. CRAFT AND STRUCTURE

2.1. KEY IDEAS AND DETAILS

2. READING: INFORMATIONAL TEXT

2.2. Craft and Structure

Common Core State Standard: CCSS.ELA-LITERACY.RI.3.4, CCSS.ELA-LITERACY.RI.3.5, CCSS.ELA-LITERACY.RI.3.6

Skills:

- Determine the meaning of general academic and domain-specific words and phrases in a text
- Use text features and search tools (e.g., key words, sidebars, hyperlinks) to locate information relevant to a given topic efficiently
- Distinguish their own point of view from that of the author of a text

=== EXAMPLE ===

EXCERPT FROM THE ARTICLE
GENERATING ENERGY FROM THE WIND

Windmills work much like wind turbines. The main difference between the two is what they are used for. Wind turbines produce electricity. Windmills were built to grind grain and pump water.

Wind turbines were first developed in the late 1800s. They were used to make electricity in Europe and North America.

This did not last long, though. Wind is **unpredictable**. It comes and goes. Sometimes there is almost no wind at all. In the 1900s, wind power was replaced by coal, oil and gas. These fuels were seen as more dependable.

E1 What does the word 'unpredictable' mean?

    A. easy to understand   **B.** hard to guess about

    C. extremelywindy   **D.** barelyvisible

Answer: **B.** The word unpredictable means "hard to predict or make a guess about."

2. READING: INFORMATIONAL TEXT

> **Directions:** *Look at the webpage and answer the questions below.*

=== EXAMPLE ===

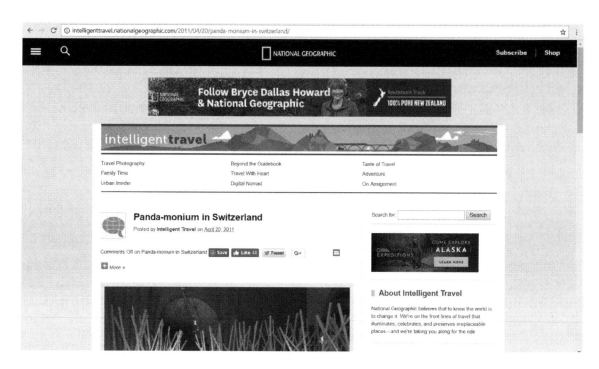

E2   What is the title of this online article? (RI.3.5)

   A. Panda-monium in Switzerland

   B. Travel Photography

   C. Intelligent Travel

   D. National Geographic

Answer: A. The title of this online article is Panda-Monium in Switzerland.

2. READING: INFORMATIONAL TEXT

> ➤ **Directions:** *Read the article and answer the questions below.*

═══════ **EXAMPLE** ═══════

THE VOICE MISSING FROM THE ELEPHANT TROPHY DEBATE? AFRICANS.

The answers for saving the Earth's wild animals seem easy from the comfortable office chairs of America and Europe. Stop hunting animals! Hunt down the poachers! More tourism!

How can we help give safe homes to wildlife? We know what the animal lovers and famous people will say. We know what the hunting groups will say. We've heard these voices before, loud and clear. But what might the people and government of Zimbabwe say? What might we hear from the people who live with elephants and lions?

People will live with wildlife only when they have some positive reason to do it. Living with elephants isn't easy. It can be dangerous. Elephants can ruin crops and even kill people. But money from tourism and even hunting can sometimes help. Often, people need it so they can keep living where they do.

Zimbabwe's population is growing very fast. Almost 2 out of 3 people there are very poor. It's already hard for them to find food. Elephants use up a lot of food and water. This makes it hard for people to live with the elephants.

Hunting can help farmers and workers. It can bring in money. It can sometimes lead to more safe areas for animals being created.

2.2. CRAFT AND STRUCTURE

E3   What is the author's point of view in this text? (RI.3.6)

A. She believes that elephant poaching can benefit the people of Africa.

B. She is against elephant poaching in Africa.

C. She believes that elephant poaching is harming the African economy.

D. She is against tourism in Africa.

Answer: A. The author believes that elephant poaching can benefit the people of Africa. She uses statistics and logical reasoning to support her argument.

Copyrighted Material   prepaze

2. READING: INFORMATIONAL TEXT

> **Directions:** *Read the passage and answer the questions below.*

BRUTAL BARRACUDAS

Did you know barracudas are deep-sea hunters? These dangerous predators have many physical features that aid them in hunting for food. Let's take a closer look at these features, what these fish eat, and how they live.

Barracudas have special physical characteristics that make them fierce. For one, they have knife-like teeth. These teeth can be used to viciously attack prey. Barracudas are also very fast. Their lightning-fast speed helps them to hunt easily. In addition to speed, they have excellent vision which helps them to carry out accurate attacks. In other words, when they go after prey, they usually do not miss.

We now know that barracudas are predators, but what do they hunt? They eat a variety of fish but may attack humans if they feel threatened. A barracuda bite can cause serious damage to human limbs. For this reason, many people are terrified of barracudas.

While many fish swim in schools, barracudas do not. These fish only unite during spawning season. At this time, they lay eggs on surface waters. At one other time during the year, barracudas unite to hunt. This is not their usual practice.

In conclusion, barracudas are known as the "Tiger of the Sea". This is because these large fish navigate the world's waters searching for their next meal.

2.2. CRAFT AND STRUCTURE

=== **MULTIPLE CHOICE** ===

1. **Read the sentence and select the best answer choice.** (RI.3.4)

   Barracudas have special <u>physical characteristics</u> that make them fierce.

   What does the phrase *physical characteristics* most likely mean in this sentence?

   A. Personalities   **B.** Body features
   C. Exercise habits   **D.** Scale colors

2. READING: INFORMATIONAL TEXT

2. **Read the sentence and select the best answer choice.** (RI.3.4)

These teeth can be used to <u>viciously</u> attack prey.

Which underlined word best replaces the word _viciously_ in this sentence?

A. These teeth can be used to <u>gently</u> attack prey.
B. These teeth can be used to <u>secretly</u> attack prey.
C. These teeth can be used to <u>violently</u> attack prey.
D. These teeth can be used to <u>gracefully</u> attack prey.

3. **Read the sentence and select the best answer choice.** (RI.3.4)

In addition to speed, they have excellent vision which helps them to carry out <u>accurate</u> attacks.

What does the word _accurate_ most likely mean in this sentence?

A. Exact   **B.** Unplanned   **C.** Unsure   **D.** Simple

4. **Read the sentence and select the best answer choice.** (RI.3.4)

These fish only unite during <u>spawning</u> season.

What does the word _spawning_ most likely mean in this sentence?

A. Hunting   **B.** Spitting   **C.** Diving   **D.** Breeding

5. **Read the sentence and select the best answer choice.** (RI.3.4)

In conclusion, barracudas are known as the "<u>tiger of the sea</u>."

What does the phrase _tiger of the sea_ most likely mean in this sentence?

A. Barracudas are wildcats that live underwater.
B. Barracudas have stripes like tigers.
C. Barracudas hunt and attack like tigers.
D. Barracudas make a tiger-like growling noise.

2.2. CRAFT AND STRUCTURE

2. READING: INFORMATIONAL TEXT

6. **Read the sentence and select the best answer choice.** (RI.3.4)

This is because these large fish <u>navigate</u> the world's waters searching for their next meal.

What does the word *navigate* most likely mean in this sentence?

A. Drive   **B.** Travel   **C.** Investigate   **D.** Pollute

7. **Which of the following would best replace the title of this text?** (RI.3.4)

A. Savage Barracudas   **B.** Aquatic Barracudas
C. Delicate Barracudas   **D.** Protective Barracudas

➤ **Directions:** *Look at the webpage and answer the questions below.*

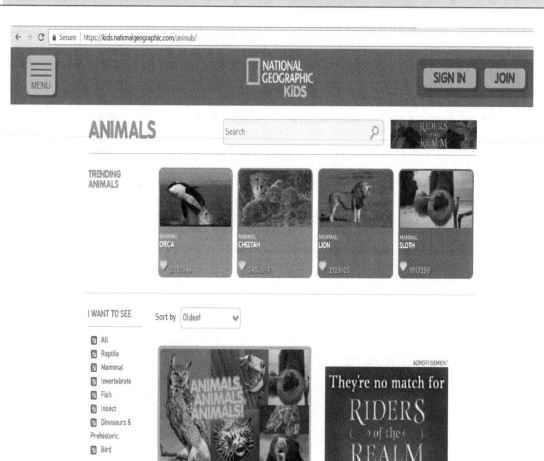

2. READING: INFORMATIONAL TEXT

=== MULTIPLE CHOICE ===

8. **What is the title of this webpage?** (RI.3.5)

A. Insects

B. Menu

C. Animals

D. Riders of the Realm

9. **How could you access information about mammals?** (RI.3.5)

A. Click on one of the boxes in the Trending Animals area.

B. Check the box next to Mammals in the I Want to See sidebar.

C. Type the word "mammals" into the search bar.

D. All of the above

10. **Where could you click to find more information about whales?** (RI.3.5)

A. Mammals: Orca

B. Mammals: Lion

C. Mammals: Sloth

D. Mammals: Cheetah

11. **What kind of information might you find if you click on the advertisement?** (RI.3.5)

A. Information about dolphins

B. Information about the novel, *Riders of the Realm*

C. Information about the website National Geographic Kids

D. Information about starting a subscription

12. **What kind of information might you find if you clicked on the menu?** (RI.3.5)

A. A list of food items

B. A list of other websites

C. A list of other topics on this website

D. None of the above

prepaze

2.2. CRAFT AND STRUCTURE

2. READING: INFORMATIONAL TEXT

13. **What kind of information would you most likely find if you clicked the "join" button?** (RI.3.5)

    A. Information about starting a subscription to receive magazines and emails

    B. Information about joining a local zoo

    C. Information about joining a local club for animal lovers

    D. Information about how lions join other pride

> **Directions:** *Read the article and answer the questions below.*

WEIGHT WATCHERS SHOULD NOT BE OFFERING ITS SERVICES TO KIDS

Many companies help people lose weight. They make billions of dollars each year. One of these companies is Weight Watchers.

Weight Watchers announced a new plan. The company will offer free services to kids as young as 13. The program begins this summer.

I am a health expert and a mother. Weight Watchers' announcement makes me angry. Kids will pay a big price for this "free" service. That's because it will make them feel bad about their bodies. It sends a message that some kids' bodies are "problems."

Weight Watchers makes people think about weight, not health. Health is more important than weight, though. Thinking only about weight can hurt people's bodies and minds.

The American Academy of Pediatrics is a group of doctors. They are experts on children's health. In 2016, they wrote a paper about diets. A diet is when someone tries to eat differently to lose weight. The paper showed that diets often have harmful effects.

One harmful effect of diets is that they can lead to eating disorders. These are diseases like anorexia and bulimia. People with anorexia feel terrified of gaining weight. They eat very little as a result. People with bulimia will eat large amounts of food. Then, they make up for it by exercising or throwing up. Eating disorders are very serious. They can even be deadly.

2.2. CRAFT AND STRUCTURE

2. READING: INFORMATIONAL TEXT

===== **MULTIPLE CHOICE** =====

14. **What issue does this article explore?** (RI.3.6)
    - **A.** The possible dangers of diets for children
    - **B.** The possible benefits of diets for children
    - **C.** The expensive cost Weight Watchers programs
    - **D.** The history of diet fads

15. **What is the author's position on this issue?** (RI.3.6)
    - **A.** Weight Watchers may be a good solution for the child obesity problem in America.
    - **B.** Weight Watchers programs should not be marketed to children.
    - **C.** Weight Watchers offers a healthy variety of foods for children.
    - **D.** Weight Watchers should be banned for both children and adults.

16. **Which of the following facts does the author use to support her argument?** (RI.3.6)
    - **A.** Weight Watchers' announcement makes me angry.
    - **B.** That's because it will make them feel bad about their bodies.
    - **C.** One harmful effect of diets is that they can lead to eating disorders.
    - **D.** Weight Watchers makes people think about weight, not health.

17. **Which of the following experts does the author mention as evidence to support her argument?** (RI.3.6)
    - **A.** A Weight Watchers representative
    - **B.** The U.S. Department of Health
    - **C.** The American Association of Dieticians
    - **D.** The American Academy of Pediatrics

2.2. CRAFT AND STRUCTURE

2. READING: INFORMATIONAL TEXT

18. **Which of the following ideas does NOT support the author's argument?** (RI.3.6)

    A. Diets can lead to eating disorders such as anorexia.

    B. Diets can promote negative body images for children.

    C. Diets can help to prevent obesity and poor health.

    D. Diets can lead to malnutrition for children.

19. **Which of the following is most likely true?** (RI.3.6)

    A. The author believes that children should focus on good health instead of weight loss.

    B. The author believes that children should explore dieting as a way to maintain good health.

    C. The author believes that Weight Watchers should be a part of school lunch programs.

    D. The author believes that Weight Watchers promotes positive self-images for children.

=== **WRITING PROMPT** ===

20. **Write a paragraph expressing your own opinion about this topic.** (RI.3.6)

_____

_____

_____

_____

_____

_____

_____

2.3. INTEGRATION OF KNOWLEDGE AND IDEAS

2.2. CRAFT AND STRUCTURE

2. READING: INFORMATIONAL TEXT

~~~ 2.3. Integration of Knowledge and Ideas ~~~

Common Core State Standard: CCSS.ELA–LITERACY.RI.3.7, CCSS.ELA–LITERACY.RI.3.8, CCSS.ELA–LITERACY.RI.3.9

Skills:

- Use information gained from illustrations (e.g., maps, photographs) and the words in a text to demonstrate an understanding
- Describe the logical connection between particular sentences and paragraphs in a text
- Compare and contrast the most important points and key details presented in two texts on the same topic.

> ➤ **Directions:** *Look at the picture and answer the questions below.*

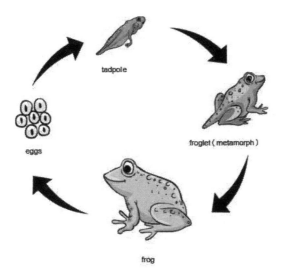

=== **MULTIPLE CHOICE** ===

E1 According to the image, a frog begins its life as (RI.3.7)

A. An egg   **B.** A froglet

C. A tadpole   **D.** A metamorph

Answer: **A.** A frog begins its life as an egg.

 prepaze

2. READING: INFORMATIONAL TEXT

===== **EXAMPLE** =====

E2   **Which of the following best describes the relationship between these two sentences?** (RI.3.8)

I fell off the bike. Now, I have a broken arm.

A. Cause and effect
B. Problem and solution
C. Sequence
D. Compare and contrast

Answer: **A.** These sentences explain how one event caused another to occur.

===== **EXAMPLE** =====

PASSAGE 1

Last summer, I visited the Grand Canyon. First, I went sightseeing. I was amazed by the breathtaking view and beautiful atmosphere. Next, I visited the historic Watchtower. The Watchtower offers a wide view that extends for nearly hundreds of miles. It was astounding! Lastly, I enjoyed hiking and rafting near the Grand Canyon. It was so much fun! These are just a few of the reasons why visiting the Grand Canyon is a wonderful experience.

PASSAGE 2

The Grand Canyon is an American national park located in the state of Arizona. It spans 18 miles across at its widest point and is about 6,000 feet deep. Although it is not the largest canyon in the world, the Grand Canyon is considered to be one of the seven wonders of the natural world. Approximately 5 million visitors flock to this popular tourist destination every year.

E2   **How are the key details similar in both texts?** (RI.3.9)
  A. Both passages describe the Watchtower.
  B. Both passages explain how the Grand Canyon was formed.
  C. Both passages offer details about the Grand Canyon.
  D. Both passages describe the Grand Canyon's size dimensions.

Answer: **C.** Both passages offer details about the Grand Canyon.

2.3. INTEGRATION OF KNOWLEDGE AND IDEAS

2. READING: INFORMATIONAL TEXT

> **Directions:** *Read each passage and look at the picture. Then answer the questions that follow.*

THE LOST SETTLEMENT OF ROANOKE

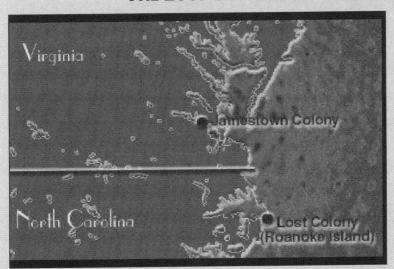

In the 1500s, Spain sent ships to the Americas. They wanted to find a new home. Sir Walter Raleigh was an important man who hoped to start a colony. When the sailors arrived in North America, they were near North Carolina. The state had not been created yet. Only Native Americans lived there. After struggling to find food and shelter, the sailors went back to England. In 1587, 115 new settlers came back. This time they created a settlement called Roanoke. One important man, John White, had to leave the other 114 men. He went back to England for supplies. Three years later, he came back to Roanoke, but the other men were gone. No one knows what happened to these men.

=== **FREE RESPONSE** ===

1. **When did Spain send ships to the Americas?** (RI.3.7)

_____

_____

_____

_____

_____

2.3. INTEGRATION OF KNOWLEDGE AND IDEAS

2. **When the men returned to Roanoke, what did they create?** (RI.3.7)

_____

_____

_____

_____

3. **According to the map, the Lost Roanoke settlement was close to what ocean?** (RI.3.7)

_____

_____

_____

4. **Why did the sailors go back to England?** (RI.3.7)

_____

_____

_____

_____

5. **According to the map, the Lost Roanoke settlement was in what state?** (RI.3.7)

_____

_____

_____

_____

2. READING: INFORMATIONAL TEXT

═══════ **MULTIPLE CHOICE** ═══════

6. **Based on the passage, which of the following events happened first?** (RI.3.7)

   A. John White went back to England.

   B. John White and the other 114 men left Roanoke.

   C. John White returned from England to find the other men had disappeared.

   D. John White and the other men arrived in the Americas.

7. **Based on the passage, which of the following events happened last?** (RI.3.7)

   A. John White went back to England to get supplies.

   B. The men came to America for the first time, searching for a better life.

   C. The 114 men disappeared.

   D. Native Americans saw the Englishmen arriving.

═══════ **MULTIPLE CHOICE** ═══════

8. **Which of the following best describes the relationship between these two sentences?** (RI.3.8)

   It started to rain outside. We decided to cancel the baseball game.

   A. Cause and effect

   B. Problem and solution

   C. Sequence

   D. Compare and contrast

9. **Which of the following sentences demonstrates problem and solution?** (RI.3.8)

   A. It is the fourth of July. We are going to watch fireworks.

   B. Emilio bought a gift for Amy. It was a stuffed teddy bear.

   C. The sun is too bright. I will wear my sunglasses.

   D. It was New Year's Eve. We stayed up late to celebrate.

2. READING: INFORMATIONAL TEXT

10. **Which of the following sentences demonstrates sequence?** (RI.3.8)

    A. First, we went to the movies, then we went to the zoo.

    B. It was extremely hot outside. We decided to go swimming.

    C. We baked chocolate chip cookies. We also baked brownies.

    D. There were mosquitos everywhere. My dad used bug spray to get rid of them.

> **Directions:** *Read the passage and answer the questions below.*

    There were two cars were in the race. One car was taller, but the other car was wider. Each car had a unique color. When the race started, the purple car zoomed into the lead. It was a lot faster than the green car. Once the purple car hit a bump, it ran off the track. The green car was slower, but it rolled a lot smoother.

=== **FREE RESPONSE** ===

11. **Explain the relationship between these sentences from the text.** (RI.3.8)

There were two cars in the race. One car was taller, but the other car was wider.

_____

_____

_____

_____

_____

_____

_____

2. READING: INFORMATIONAL TEXT

12. **Explain how these sentences demonstrate cause and effect.** (RI.3.8)

Once the purple car hit a bump, it ran off the track.

_____

_____

_____

_____

_____

_____

➢ **Directions:** *Read the passages and answer the questions below.*

PASSAGE 1
PLANTS GROWING IN THE AMAZON RAINFOREST

The largest forest in the world is filled with life. There are so many different kinds of plants that those plants commonly seen in the United States seem boring and dull. Travel with me as we explore the secrets found in the Amazon Rainforest.

There are many types of plants found in the Amazon Rainforest. Some of these plants are used to make medicine. In fact, many scientists believe that the key to curing cancer is inside a plant growing in the rainforest. Scientists spend a lot of time studying these plants growing in South America.

2.3. INTEGRATION OF KNOWLEDGE AND IDEAS

prepaze

2. READING: INFORMATIONAL TEXT

PASSAGE 2
TREES OF THE AMAZON RAINFOREST

The Amazon Rainforest is located in South America. It is over 2 million square miles. Covering a lot of Brazil and parts of Colombia, Peru, and some other South American countries, this is the world's biggest tropical rainforest. Inside this lively area, there are many fascinating trees. Did you know that trees in the Amazon Rainforest are very useful? Perhaps, their most important job is providing oxygen. Over twenty percent of the world's oxygen is produced in the Amazon Rainforest.

=== TRUE OR FALSE ===

13. **Both passages present information about the Amazon Rainforest.** (RI.3.9)

    A. True   **B.** False

14. **Both passages present information about how plants from the Amazon Rainforest are used to make medicine.** (RI.3.9)

    A. True   **B.** False

15. **Passage 1 offers more geographical information about the Amazon Rainforest than passage 2.** (RI.3.9)

    A. True   **B.** False

16. **Passage 1 focuses more on the production of oxygen in the Amazon Rainforest than passage 2.** (RI.3.9)

    A. True   **B.** False

17. **Both passages explain how the Amazon Rainforest is useful to humans.** (RI.3.9)

    A. True   **B.** False

2. READING: INFORMATIONAL TEXT

=== **MULTIPLE CHOICE** ===

18. **Which of these key points is presented in passage 1?** (RI.3.9)

   A. Over twenty percent of the world's oxygen is produced in the Amazon Rainforest.

   B. There are many types of plants found in the Amazon Rainforest.

   C. It is over 2 million square miles.

   D. Inside this lively area, there are many fascinating trees.

19. **Which of these key points is presented in passage 2?** (RI.3.9)

   A. There are so many different kinds of plants that those plants commonly seen in the United States seem boring and dull.

   B. Some of these plants are used to make medicine.

   C. In fact, many scientists believe that the key to curing cancer is inside a plant growing in the rainforest.

   D. Covering a lot of Brazil and parts of Colombia, Peru, and some other South American countries, this is the world's biggest tropical rainforest.

20. **Which of these key points is presented in both passages?** (RI.3.9)

   A. The Amazon Rainforest is located in South America.

   B. The Amazon Rainforest has many useful plants.

   C. The Amazon Rainforest has many useful trees.

   D. The Amazon Rainforest is the world's biggest rainforest.

2.3. INTEGRATION OF KNOWLEDGE AND IDEAS

2.4. CHAPTER REVIEW ▷▷▷

2.4. Chapter Review

2.4. CHAPTER REVIEW

> ➢ **Directions:** *Read the passage and answer the questions below.*

SPACECRAFT INSIGHT'S MISSION IS TO FIND CLUES ON HOW MARS FIRST FORMED

The spacecraft launched early on the morning of Saturday, May 5. It carries tools to take the temperature and measure shakes deep beneath Mars' surface. Even the slightest shake could carry clues about how the planet formed. Scientists will also learn what goes on today beneath the planet's surface.

Suzanne Smrekar is a NASA scientist working on the project. She said one reason Earth looks different from Mars is plate tectonics. Plate tectonics means that the outer layer of the Earth is made from separate pieces, or plates. They move very slowly over time. As they move, they reshape the continents, creating volcanoes and causing earthquakes.

The spacecraft will travel for six months. The journey to Mars will cover 300 million miles. You could go to the moon and back more than 600 times in the distance of this one Mars trip.

The results might be the key to a four-billion-year-old mystery. Scientists believe that Mars used to have a magnetic field like Earth. The field was created by Mars' core and the other layers of the planet. That field probably protected the planet. Back then, Mars was a warm, wet place, with oceans whose shorelines can still be seen today. That planet and ours may have been nearly twins.

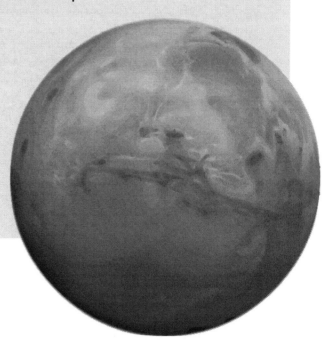

2. READING: INFORMATIONAL TEXT

=== **MULTIPLE CHOICE** ===

1. **Read the sentence and select the best answer choice.** (RI.3.4)

   The <u>spacecraft</u> launched early on the morning of Saturday, May 5.

   What does the word *spacecraft* most likely mean in this sentence?
   A. A project in outer space
   B. A vehicle used for traveling into outer space
   C. An astronaut
   D. A planet

2. **Read the sentences and select the best answer choice.** (RI.3.4)

   She said one reason Earth looks different from Mars is <u>plate tectonics</u>.

   What does the phrase *plate tectonics* most likely mean in this sentence?
   A. The structure of the Earth's layers
   B. The study of electronic plates in outer space
   C. The structure of electronic spacecraft
   D. The study of gravity on Earth

3. **Read the sentence and select the best answer choice.** (RI.3.4)

   Scientists believe that Mars used to have a <u>magnetic field</u> like Earth.

   What does the phrase *magnetic field* most likely mean in this sentence?
   A. A field of magnets
   B. An area that looks like a magnet
   C. An area of magnetic force
   D. None of the above

2. READING: INFORMATIONAL TEXT

4.   Read the sentence and select the best answer choice. (RI.3.4)

Back then, Mars was a warm, wet place, with oceans whose <u>shorelines</u> can still be seen today.

What does the word *shorelines* most likely mean in this sentence?

A. Lines drawn on a map

B. Oceans with lines drawn in them

C. Natural lines that separate oceans and shores, or land

D. Imaginary lines that separate planets in outer space

> **Directions:** *Read the passage and answer the questions below.*

POPULAR REWARDS PROGRAM: GOOD FOR SCHOOLS, BAD FOR KIDS?

Labels-for-cash programs are popular. Many schools take part in them. In these programs, students and parents clip special labels from packages of food. It may be a bag of cookies or a box of cereal.

Schools collect these special labels. They send them to the food company. The school gets money in return.

School workers like these programs. They help raise extra money. The school can use it to buy supplies. They may buy pencils, markers or even playground toys.

Health experts feel differently. They do not like these programs at all. They say label programs are just a way to sell junk food to kids.

The programs include snack foods, like cookies. Health workers say these foods are not good for kids. They think label programs teach unhealthy eating. They encourage families to buy these foods. Families do it to help raise money for their school. But at the same time, they are giving kids unhealthy foods.

2. READING: INFORMATIONAL TEXT

=== **MULTIPLE CHOICE** ===

5. **What is the issue being discussed in this text?** (RI.3.6)
   A. Schools are selling junk food in vending machines.
   B. Food companies are offering schools money in exchange for junk food labels.
   C. Students are eating too much junk food during lunch.
   D. Food companies are running out of money used for school fundraisers.

6. **What is the author's position on this issue?** (RI.3.6)
   A. Labels-for-cash programs are not making enough money.
   B. Labels-for-cash programs can raise money but may promote unhealthy food habits.
   C. Labels-for-cash programs should be included in more school fundraisers.
   D. Labels-for-cash programs should be used to buy more school supplies.

7. **Which of the following facts does the author use to support the argument in this text?** (RI.3.6)
   A. Health experts say that label programs are just a way to sell junk food to kids.
   B. Teachers say that label programs help them to buy classroom supplies.
   C. School officials say that the label programs promote health and nutrition in schools.
   D. Health experts say that the label programs help to raise money for physical education.

prepaze

2. READING: INFORMATIONAL TEXT

=== **WRITING PROMPT** ===

8.   **Write a paragraph about your opinion on this topic.** (RI.3.6)

_____

_____

_____

_____

_____

_____

_____

_____

_____

_____

_____

_____

2.4. CHAPTER REVIEW

> ➤   **Directions:** *Read the text and answer the questions below.*

THE 3 R'S: REDUCE, REUSE, RECYCLE

     Have you ever heard of the three R's? They are reduced, reuse, and recycle. These actions should be practiced in our daily life. Taken together they will limit the amount of waste we make on a daily basis. It is important to practice them in our lives to help our environment. A great place to start practicing the three R's is in the classroom. To reduce waste, we can take the minimal amount of supplies we need.

...continued next page

2. READING: INFORMATIONAL TEXT

By doing so, we will not have leftover materials that go to waste. We can also reduce waste in the cafeteria. We can bring a lunch box instead of throwing brown paper bags away in the trash. Bringing a drink in a reusable water bottle helps, too. We can reuse reading books by carefully wrapping them with paper. By covering the books, they can remain scratch free and be reused again next year. We can recycle the paper and plastic materials we use after they are no longer needed. Instead of throwing away our empty glue bottles, ink cartridges, and binders in a landfill, we can recycle them. Practicing the three R's will help save money, energy, and natural resources. If we practice the three R's in the classroom, we can make a big difference in helping our planet.

TRUE OR FALSE

9. **The phrase reduce, review, and recycle is known as the three R's.** (RI.3.1)

   A. True

   B. False

10. **According to the text, we should reduce, reuse, and recycle once every year.** (RI.3.1)

    A. True

    B. False

11. **If we reduce, reuse, and recycle, we will limit the amount of waste we make.** (RI.3.1)

    A. True

    B. False

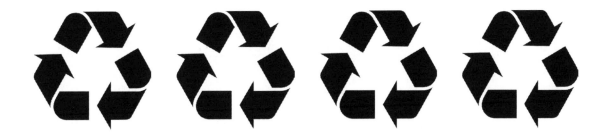

prepaze

=== **FREE RESPONSE** ===

12. **According to the text, how can books be reused?** (RI.3.1)

_____

_____

_____

_____

_____

_____

_____

_____

_____

_____

_____

_____

_____

_____

_____

2. 4. CHAPTER REVIEW

2. READING: INFORMATIONAL TEXT

> ➤ **Directions:** *Look at the picture and answer the questions below.*

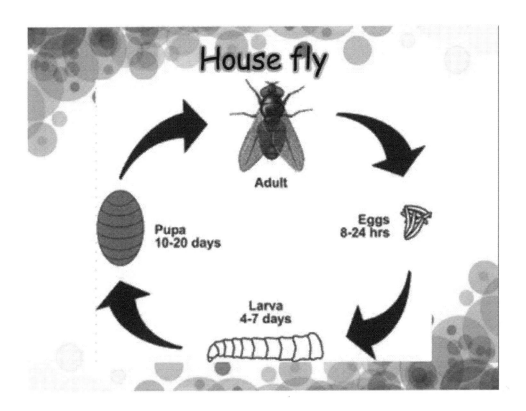

13. **What is the shortest amount of time it will take for a house fly to reach the larva stage?** (RI.3.7)

    A. 8 days   **B.** 4 days   **C.** 10 hours   **D.** 8 hours

14. **After completing the larval stage, a house fly begins which stage:** (RI.3.7)

    A. Pupa   **B.** Adult
    C. Eggs   **D.** None of the above

15. **Based on the picture, the house fly spends the least amount of time as** (RI.3.7)

    A. An egg   **B.** Pupa   **C.** Larva   **D.** An adult

2. READING: INFORMATIONAL TEXT

> **Directions:** *Read the passage and answer the questions below.*

COMPOSTING

Not everything we throw away is trash. It is important to reuse plant and food waste by composting it. This helps us to have less garbage to throw away. By reusing the waste, landfills will fill up more slowly, and we can help the Earth. Composting lets things decompose or break down on their own. We combine dead leaves, grass clippings, fruit and vegetable peels into a pile. We then mix this waste with soil until everything breaks down. This is nature's way of reusing the waste. We toss the food scraps and yard waste into an open bin outside. The compost pile soaks up water so that the materials inside the bin will decay. When the pile is stirred, the materials will have more air and decompose faster. When there is air and water, the tiny animals in the soil break the waste into small pieces. The pile of waste adds nutrients to the soil. This soil can then be spread on gardens to grow plants. Compost acts as a natural fertilizer. It helps the plants grow without adding any harmful chemicals.

=== **FREE RESPONSE** ===

16. **What is the main topic of the text?** (RI.3.2)

_____

_____

_____

_____

_____

_____

prep@ze   **www.prepaze.com**

2. READING: INFORMATIONAL TEXT

17. **How is the main topic supported by key details? List at least 3 details.** (RI.3.2)

_____

_____

_____

_____

_____

_____

_____

_____

_____

_____

_____

_____

_____

_____

_____

prepaze

2. READING: INFORMATIONAL TEXT

> ➢ **Directions:** *Look at the webpage and answer the questions below.*

If spiders worked together, they could eat all humans in a year

By Chris Murphy, The Sun   March 29, 2017 | 12:30pm

Getty Images

ORIGINALLY PUBLISHED BY:

One robot can more than six humans out of a job

Ikea has designed mobile lightbulbs that hackers could hijack

World's largest dinosaur footprint discovered in Australia

Mysterious 2,300-year-old palace discovered in Mexico

Humans beware: if the world's present population of spiders ever get organized, they could eat us all in just 12 months.

That's the shock new finding from a piece of research that is set to give everyone nightmares.

At the moment, spiders mostly eat insects, although some of the larger species have been known to snack on lizards, birds and even small mammals.

But in a report published in the Washington Post, experts said that if you add up the weight of all the food eaten by the world's entire spider population in a single year is more than the combined weight of every human on the planet.

Martin Nyffeler of the University of Basel in Switzerland and Klaus Birkhofer of Lund University in Sweden and the Brandenburg University of Technology Cottbus-Senftenberg in Germany, published their findings in the journal Science of Nature this month.

They discovered spiders across the globe consume between 440.9 and 881.8 million tons of prey in any given year.

prepaze   **www.prepaze.com**

2. READING: INFORMATIONAL TEXT

18. **What is the topic of this article?** (RI.3.5)

    A. Spiders can work together to consume humans.

    B. The net weight of insects consumed yearly by the world's spiders is greater than the combined net weight of living humans.

    C. The net weight of insects consumed yearly by the world's spiders indicates that spiders may one day be capable of consuming humans.

    D. Spiders cannot work together to consume mammals.

19. **Who is the author of this article?** (RI.3.5)

    A. The Sun   **B.** Getty

    C. Living Magazine   **D.** Chris Murphy

20. **Who is the publisher of this article?** (RI.3.5)

    A. Living Magazine

    B. Getty Images

    C. The Sun

    D. Chris Murphy

> **Directions:** *Read the passage and answer the questions below.*

PASSAGE 1
PLANTS GROWING IN THE AMAZON RAINFOREST

The Foxglove is one plant that is used to make medicine. This plant can help people with their heart problems. Since heart conditions are a problem for many people, the foxglove plant is very important.

The Trillium is another important plant. It grows in the Amazon Rainforest too. This plant can be used to treat snake bites. Wow! How wonderful is it that these plants are growing and ready to be discovered?

Clearly, the rainforest is filled with many important plants. These plants will continue to change people's lives and make them healthier and stronger.

...continued next page

 prepaze

2. 4. CHAPTER REVIEW

2. READING: INFORMATIONAL TEXT

PASSAGE 2
TREES OF THE AMAZON RAINFOREST

Trees inside the Amazon Rainforest are used for many necessary items. Have you ever heard of rubber tappers? These people work very hard to tap the rubber in trees. This is done by cutting slips in the trees. As the sap drips out, it is collected. As rubber tappers do this, the trees are not hurt at all. After being harvested, the rubber is used to make many useful items, including car tires and erasers.

Items containing rubber are only one type of product created using this rainforest's gifts. The wood from the trees can be turned into paper. Many huge logging companies harvest trees that are used to make many beautiful household items. By harvesting rosewood, mahogany, oak, and tea, floorboards and furniture are created. People love having items created from these exotic woods because of their beauty and luster.

=== **FILL IN THE BLANK** ===

21. **Both passages explain how resources from the _____ are used to make other things.** (RI.3.9)

22. **Passage _____ explains how plants are used to make medicine.** (RI.3.9)

23. **Passage _____ explains how trees are used to make rubber.** (RI.3.9)

2. READING: INFORMATIONAL TEXT

> **Directions:** *Read the passage and answer the questions.*

FAMOUS U.S. PRESIDENTS

George Washington and Abraham Lincoln are two of the most famous presidents in U.S. history. Because of their contributions to our country, they are both observed on U.S. currency and Mount Rushmore. They are also honored with the Lincoln Memorial and Washington Monument.

In 1775, Washington was elected Commander in Chief of the Continental Army. He served during the American Revolutionary War. In 1787, he led the Constitutional Convention that drafted the U.S. Constitution. He was one of the Founding Fathers of the United States. Washington was the first President of the United States, serving two terms from 1789 to 1797.

Abraham Lincoln was the 16th president. He served from March 1861 until his assassination in April 1865. He led the Union Army to victory during the Civil War. He fought to unite the country and end slavery. On January 1, 1863, he issued the Emancipation Proclamation. It gave freedom to slaves in states rebelling against the Union.

=== **MULTIPLE CHOICE** ===

24. What happened as a result of Washington and Lincoln's contributions to the United States? (RI.3.3)

   A. They are honored with monuments and currency.

   B. They were elected as presidents.

   C. They led American wars.

   D. They served presidential terms.

25. Which event happened first? (RI.3.3)

   A. Abraham Lincoln was the 16th president.

   B. Washington was the first President of the United States, serving two terms from 1789 to 1797.

   C. In 1775, Washington was elected Commander in Chief of the Continental Army.

   D. On January 1, 1863, he issued the Emancipation Proclamation.

2. READING: INFORMATIONAL TEXT

=== **FREE RESPONSE** ===

26. Explain how Abraham Lincoln's presidency affected slavery. (RI.3.3)

_____

_____

_____

_____

_____

_____

_____

_____

27. Which of the following sentences demonstrate problem and solution? (RI.3.8)

A. She spilled milk on the table. She cleaned it up with a towel.

B. We had a flat tire. I fixed it.

C. His pencil lead was broken. He used a pencil sharpener to fix it.

D. All of the above

28. Which of the following sentences demonstrate cause and effect? (RI.3.8)

A. He works as a cashier. He is also a painter.

B. The wind blew violently. It knocked the tree down.

C. First I chopped the onions. Then I peeled the potatoes.

D. None of the sentences demonstrate cause and effect.

2. READING: INFORMATIONAL TEXT

=== **WRITING PROMPT** ===

29. **Imagine that you just got a new pet. Write a paragraph that describes what happened when you brought the pet home. Use transitional words (first, then, finally, etc.) to put the events in the order in which they happened.** (RI.3.8)

_____

_____

_____

_____

_____

30. **Think of your favorite food. Now, think of your least favorite food. Write a paragraph that compares these two foods. Use words such as least, better, similar, etc. in order to show comparison.** (RI.3.8)

_____

_____

_____

_____

_____

2.4. CHAPTER REVIEW

prepaze

3. READING: FOUNDATIONAL SKILLS

3. READING: FOUNDATIONAL SKILLS

~~~~~ 3.1. Phonics and Word Recognition ~~~~~

Common Core State Standards: CCSS.ELA-LITERACY.RF.3.3.A, CCSS.ELA-LITERACY.RF.3.3.B, CCSS.ELA-LITERACY.RF.3.3.C, CCSS.ELA-LITERACY.RF.3.3.D

Skills:

- Know and apply grade-level phonics and word analysis skills in decoding words.
- Identify and know the meaning of the most common prefixes and derivational suffixes
- Decode words with common Latin suffixes
- Decode multisyllable words.
- Read grade-appropriate irregularly spelled words.

===== **EXAMPLE** =====

E1   Which of these words mean "to view or look at again?" (RF.3.3.A)

    A. preview   **B.** review   **C.** viewer   **D.** viewing

Correct Answer: B. The prefix re- means "again." The word *review* means "to view or look at again."

E2   Which of these words mean "can be folded?" (RF.3.3.B)

    A. folder   **B.** unfold   **C.** foldable   **D.** refold

Correct Answer: C. The suffix -able means "able to" or "can be or do." The word *foldable* means "can be folded."

E3   Which of these words has 3 syllables? (RF.3.3.C)

    A. family   **B.** dragon   **C.** tenth   **D.** pillow

Correct Answer: C. The word *family* has 3 syllables. A syllable is a single unit of sound that has one vowel sound. The word *family* is divided into three syllables (fam + i + ly).

3.1. PHONICS AND WORD RECOGNITION

prepaze   **www.prepaze.com**

3. READING: FOUNDATIONAL SKILLS

E4 **Which of these words has an irregular spelling?** (RF.3.3.D)

    A. pouch   **B.** bedroom   **C.** spider   **D.** height

Correct Answer: **C.** The word *height* has an irregular spelling. Irregularly spelled words have letters that make an unusual sound. In the word *height* the vowel blend *ei* makes the long /i/ sound and the consonant blend *gh* is silent.

> ➢ **Directions:** *Read the question and select the best answer choice.*

=== **MULTIPLE CHOICE** ===

1. **Which of these words means "a person who teaches?"** (RF.3.3.A, RF.3.3.B)

    A. teachable   **B.** teaching   **C.** teacher   **D.** teaches

2. **Which of these words means "in a mild way?"** (RF.3.3.A, RF.3.3.B)

    A. mildest   **B.** mildly   **C.** milder   **D.** mild

3. **Which of these words means "without hope?"** (RF.3.3.A)

    A. hopeful   **B.** hopeless   **C.** hopefully   **D.** hoping

4. **What is the meaning of the underlined word?** (RF.3.3.A)

    He would never <u>disobey</u> the rules in school.

    A. to not obey   **B.** to fully obey
    C. able to obey   **D.** to obey again

5. **Which of these suffixes means "having or made of?"** (RF.3.3.A)

    A. -less   **B.** -ful   **C.** -er   **D.** -y

3.1. PHONICS AND WORD RECOGNITION

3. READING: FOUNDATIONAL SKILLS

> **Directions:** *Circle the correct word in each sentence.*

3. 1. PHONICS AND WORD RECOGNITION

6.   **Read the sentence. Circle the word with an irregular spelling.** (RF.3.3.D)

Chad will surely win the cooking contest.

7.   **Read the sentence. Circle the word with 3 syllables.** (RF.3.3.C)

He is a very talented baker and chef.

8.   **Read the sentence. Circle the word(s) that have a suffix meaning "having or made of."** (RF.3.3.A)

Chad will make a spicy chicken salad with crunchy lettuce.

═══════════════ **TRUE OR FALSE** ═══════════════

9.   **The word *exam* is an irregularly spelled word.** (RF.3.3.D)
   A. True   **B.** False

10. **The word *almost* has 3 syllables.** (RF.3.3.C)
   A. True   **B.** False

11. **The Latin suffix -or means "in a certain way."** (RF.3.3.B)
   A. True   **B.** False

12. **The double consonant ss makes the /sh/ sound in the word *mission*.** (RF.3.3.D)
   A. True   **B.** False

13. **There are 2 vowel sounds in each syllable of a word.** (RF.3.3.C)
   A. True   **B.** False

3. READING: FOUNDATIONAL SKILLS

> **Directions:** *Read the question and select the best answer choice.*

=== **MULTIPLE CHOICE** ===

14. **How many syllables are there in the word *watermelon?*** (RF.3.3.C)

    A. 4   **B.** 1   **C.** 3   **D.** 2

15. **What is the correct way to divide the word *yesterday* into syllables?** (RF.3.3.C)

    A. ye + ster + day   **B.** yes + ter + day
    C. yester + day   **D.** y + est + er + day

16. **Which letters make an unusual sound in the word *conquer?*** (RF.3.3.D)

    A. er   **B.** con   **C.** qu   **D.** ue

> **Directions:** *Rewrite the sentence by adding a prefix or suffix to the underlined word.*

=== **FREE RESPONSE** ===

17. **Add the best prefix to the underlined word.** (RF.3.3.A)

    It is very <u>safe</u> to ride a bike without a helmet.

    _____

18. **Add the best suffix to the underlined word.** (RF.3.3.A)

    She looked <u>fear</u> as she bravely climbed the mountain.

    _____

3.1. PHONICS AND WORD RECOGNITION

prepaze

3. READING: FOUNDATIONAL SKILLS

19. Add the Latin suffix meaning "in a certain way" to the underlined word. (RF.3.3.B)

She <u>quick</u> ran away from the angry dog.

_____

20. Add the prefix meaning "before" to the underlined word. (RF.3.3.A)

The first step is to <u>heat</u> the oven. The next step is to make the dough.

_____

3.1. PHONICS AND WORD RECOGNITION

3.2. CHAPTER REVIEW

3. READING: FOUNDATIONAL SKILLS

~~~~ 3.2. Chapter Review ~~~~

> ➤ **Directions:** *Read the passage and answer the questions below.*

CLIMBING WILL NO LONGER BE ALLOWED ON ULURU

Starting in the 1950s, Uluru became a tourist destination. There is a fancy resort nearby. Tour buses bring **visitors** daily. Climbing the rock has been a favorite **activity**. Next year, though, **climbing** will be banned.

Uluru is sacred to the Anangu people. They are Aboriginal people — the first people to live in Australia. These people lived in Australia before anyone else. The Anangu never wanted tourists to climb Uluru. For them, climbing up Uluru is like climbing a church or other place of **worship**. It is very **disrespectful.** They put up signs that said: Please Don't Climb. Only some people respected those wishes, though.

=== MULTIPLE CHOICE ===

1. **What is the meaning of the word *visitors?*** (RF.3.3.A, RF.3.3.B)

   A. full of visits
   C. having visits
   B. people who visit
   D. without visits

2. **What is the meaning of the word *disrespectful?*** (RF.3.3.A)

   A. very respectful
   C. not respectful
   B. person who is respectful
   D. to be respectful again

3. **How many syllables are there in the word *activity?*** (RF.3.3.C)

   A. 3   **B.** 2   **C.** 1   **D.** 4

4. **Which of these words has an irregular spelling?** (RF.3.3.D)

   A. climbing
   C. activity
   B. disrespectful
   D. visitors

3. READING: FOUNDATIONAL SKILLS

5. **Which of these letters make an unusual sound in the word *worship*?** (RF.3.3.D)

   A. sh   **B.** r   **C.** or   **D.** w

> **Directions:** *Read the passage and answer the questions below.*

CLIMBING WILL NO LONGER BE ALLOWED ON ULURU

In recent years, fewer tourists have climbed Uluru. Anangu **leaders** and park **officials** made a decision. They agreed to ban climbing. The Anangu people cheered the new rule. The ban goes into effect in October 2019.

The Anangu people still want tourists to visit. Their **community** has very little money. Tourism is their main source of income. Tourists come to Uluru and spend a lot. They stay in expensive hotels and eat at nice restaurants. They take bike and bus tours.

=== TRUE OR FALSE ===

6. **The word *leaders* means "people who lead."** (RF.3.3.A)

   A. True   **B.** False

7. **The word *officials* is a regularly spelled word.** (RF.3.3.D)

   A. True   **B.** False

8. **The word *community* has 3 syllables.** (RF.3.3.C)

   A. True   **B.** False

3. READING: FOUNDATIONAL SKILLS

> **Directions:** *Circle the correct word in each sentence.*

9. **Read the sentence. Circle the word with an irregular spelling.** (RF.2.3.D)

    Tropical birds prefer to live in sunny regions.

10. **Read the sentence. Circle the word with a Latin suffix.** (RF.2.3.B)

    The flamingo bird has a long, flexible neck.

11. **Read the sentence. Circle the word with the prefix that means "again."** (RF.2.3.B)

    A parrot can repeat sounds from the environment.

12. **Read the sentence. Circle the words with 3 syllables** (RF.2.3.C)

    A toucan has a long, colorful beak that is used for hunting.

> **Directions:** *Choose the word that best completes the sentence.*

=== **MULTIPLE CHOICE** ===

13. **A _____ is a single unit of sound in a word.** (RF.3.3.C)
    A. syllable **B.** suffix **C.** prefix **D.** spelling

14. **There is/are _____ vowel sound(s) in each syllable of a word.** (RF.3.3.C)
    A. two **B.** one **C.** three **D.** many

15. **A _____ can be added to the beginning of a word to change its meaning.** (RF.3.3.A)
    A. suffix **B.** syllable **C.** prefix **D.** base word

 prepaze

16. A(n) _____ spelled word has letters that make unusual sounds. (RF.3.3.C)

    A. regularly   **B.** irregularly   **C.** correctly   **D.** incorrectly

> ➢ **Directions:** *Rewrite the sentence by adding a prefix or suffix to the underlined word.*

═══════════════════ **FREE RESPONSE** ═══════════════════

17. **Add the best suffix to the underlined word.** (RF.3.3.A)

A dictionary can be <u>help</u> when learning new words.

_____

18. **Add the best Latin suffix to the underlined word.** (RF.3.3.A, RF.3.3.B)

The <u>act</u> took a bow at the end of the play.

_____

19. **Add a prefix that changes the underlined word to its opposite meaning.** (RF.3.3.A)

The clouds seem to <u>appear</u> at night.

_____

20. **Add a suffix that changes the underlined word to mean "having or made of."** (RF.3.3.A)

The pudding was smooth and <u>cream</u>.

_____

3. READING: FOUNDATIONAL SKILLS

> **Directions:** *Read the question and select the best answer choice.*

=== **MULTIPLE CHOICE** ===

21. **Which of these words has an irregular spelling?** (RF.3.3.D)

    A. special **B.** spotted **C.** speck **D.** spoonful

22. **Which of these words does not have an irregular spelling?** (RF.3.3.D)

    A. dessert **B.** division **C.** design **D.** dentist

23. **Which of these words has a Latin suffix?** (RF.3.3.B)

    A. wonderful **B.** careless **C.** adorable **D.** funny

24. **Which of these words means "a person who speaks?"** (RF.3.3.A)

    A. speaking **B.** speaker **C.** speechless **D.** spoken

25. **Which of these words means "in a silent way?"** (RF.3.3.A)

    A. silently **B.** silence **C.** silent **D.** unsilent

26. **Which of these words has 4 syllables?** (RF.3.3.C)

    A. photograph **B.** ambulance **C.** alligator **D.** mountain

27. **What is the correct way to divide the word *rocketship* into syllables?** (RF.3.3.C)

    A. rocket + ship   **B.** rock + et + ship
    C. ro + ck + et + ship   **D.** roc + ket + ship

28. **What is the correct way to divide the word *motorboat* into syllables?** (RF.3.3.C)

    A. mo + to + rboat   **B.** mot + or + boat
    C. motor + boat   **D.** mo + tor + boat

3.2. CHAPTER REVIEW

 prepaze

3. READING: FOUNDATIONAL SKILLS

29. **Which of these consonants make an unusual sound in the word *business*?** (RF.3.3.D)

    A. b   **B.** n   **C.** s   **D.** ss

30. **Which of these words has a vowel blend that makes an unusual sound?** (RF.3.3.D)

    A. hearty   **B.** peer   **C.** mouthful   **D.** moonlight

3. 2. CHAPTER REVIEW

4. WRITING

4. WRITING

4.1. Text Types and Purpose

Common Core State Standard: CCSS.ELA-LITERACY.W.3.1, CCSS.ELA-LITERACY.W.3.2, CCSS.ELA-LITERACY.W.3.3

Skills:

- Write opinion pieces on topics or texts, supporting a point of view with reasons
- Introduce the topic or text
- Provide reasons that support the opinion
- Use linking words and phrases
- Provide a concluding statement or section
- Write informative/explanatory texts to examine a topic and convey ideas and information clearly
- Introduce a topic and group related information together
- Develop the topic with facts, definitions, and details
- Use linking words and phrases
- Provide a concluding statement or section
- Write narratives to develop real or imagined experiences or events
- Establish a situation and introduce a narrator and/or characters
- Use dialogue and descriptions of actions, thoughts, and feelings to develop experiences and events
- Use temporal words and phrases to signal event order
- Provide a sense of closure

4.1. TEXT TYPES AND PURPOSE

4. WRITING

> **Directions:** *Read the question and select the best answer choice.*

======= **EXAMPLE** =======

E1 **Your teacher tells you to write about your favorite holiday. What style of writing is your teacher asking you to write?** (w.3.1)

A. Opinion
B. Informative/Explanatory
C. Narrative
D. Descriptive

Answer: **A.** Because the teacher is asking you to express which holiday you like the best, you are being asked to write an opinion piece.

E2 **Your teacher tells you to write about the history of Mount Rushmore. What style of writing is your teacher asking you to write?** (w.3.1)

A. Opinion
B. Informative/Explanatory
C. Narrative
D. Descriptive

Answer: **B.** Because the teacher is asking you to write about the history of Mount Rushmore, which will require you to include facts about the monument, you are being asked to write an informative/explanatory text.

E3 **Your teacher tells you to write a story about your experience on a field trip. What style of writing is this?** (w.3.1)

A. Opinion
B. Informative/Explanatory
C. Narrative
D. Descriptive

Answer: **C.** Because the teacher is asking you to write about your experience on a field trip, you are detailing a real experience that happened to you, this means you are being asked to write a narrative story.

4.1. TEXT TYPES AND PURPOSE

prepaze

4. WRITING

═══════════════ **TRUE OR FALSE** ═══════════════

1. **Opinion pieces are based on fact or knowledge about a topic or text.** (W.3.1)

   A. True   **B.** False

2. **When you write an opinion piece, you give your point of view on a topic and support your opinion with a list of reasons.** (W.3.1.B)

   A. True   **B.** False

═══════════════ **MULTIPLE CHOICE** ═══════════════

3. **You wrote the sentence, "Dogs make great pets, therefore all people should have them as a pet." The word "therefore" is a:** (W.3.1.C)

   A. Noun   **B.** Linking word
   C. Concluding statement   **D.** Verb

4. **Which of the following sentences would work best when introducing a topic for an opinion piece?** (W.3.1.A)

   A. "My point of view on this is..."
   B. "My life started..."
   C. "My dad took me on a trip to..."
   D. "My dog's name is Billy and he..."

5. **You are assigned to write an opinion piece about your favorite U.S. President. Which of the following statements would work best?** (W.3.1)

   A. President Washington was the only president to never live in the White House.
   B. President Roosevelt had lots of pets in the White House.
   C. President Lincoln was a good man who wanted to unite the country.
   D. President Reagan liked to eat jellybeans.

4. WRITING

6. **Which of the following would work best as a concluding statement?** (W.3.1.D)

   A. To summarize, summer is the best season for surfing.

   B. First of all, the beaches are more fun in the summer.

   C. Also, people get sunburn most commonly in the summer.

   D. Next, we went to the beach to go surfing.

7. **Which of the following would not work as an introductory statement?** (W.3.1.A)

   A. To begin, football is more entertaining than baseball.

   B. First, you should always wear protective gear when playing football.

   C. As you can see, I have listed many reasons why football is an unsafe sport.

   D. For example, football players are much faster than baseball players.

   ===== **WRITING PROMPT** =====

8. **Write an opinion piece about your favorite movie.** (W.3.1)

   _____

   _____

   _____

   _____

   _____

   _____

   _____

   _____

4.1. TEXT TYPES AND PURPOSE

prepaze

4. WRITING

_____

_____

_____

_____

_____

_____

_____

4.1. TEXT TYPES AND PURPOSE

=== **MULTIPLE CHOICE** ===

9. **You wrote the sentence, "Cheetahs can run up to 75 mph, but they can only run that fast for a short period of time." The word "but" is a:** (W.3.2.C)

   A. Noun
   B. Linking word
   C. Concluding statement
   D. Verb

10. **You are assigned to write an informative text about rainbows. Which of the following statements would work best?** (W.3.2.B)

   A. Rainbows are fun to look at after a rainstorm.
   B. Rainbows have many pretty colors.
   C. Stories tell us there is a pot of gold at the end of a rainbow.
   D. Rainbows are made from sunlight that passes through water.

11. **Which of the following sentence openers would work best when introducing a topic for an informative text?** (W.3.2.A)

   A. "Baseball is the greatest sport to play..."
   B. "On my first day of work..."
   C. "All people should learn to play piano because..."
   D. "The Star-Spangled Banner is America's national anthem ..."

4. WRITING

===== **TRUE OR FALSE** =====

12. **If you were writing about how to make candles, you would be writing an explanatory text.** (W.3.2)

    A. True   **B.** False

13. **Informative texts are based on facts, definitions, and details.** (W.3.2.B)

    A. True   **B.** False

14. **You wrote a sentence that says, "In conclusion, nearly 70 percent of the Earth is covered by water." This is an example of an introductory statement.** (W.3.2.A, W.3.2.D)

    A. True   **B.** False

===== **WRITING PROMPT** =====

15. **Write an explanatory text about how to get good grades in school.** (W.3.2)

    _____

    _____

    _____

    _____

    _____

    _____

    _____

    _____

    _____

 prepaze

4. WRITING

=== **MULTIPLE CHOICE** ===

16. **You wrote the sentence, "After the final bell rang, the school children cheered." The word "after" is a:** (W.3.3.C)

    A. Noun

    B. Linking word

    C. Temporal word

    D. Verb

17. **You are assigned to write a narrative about three characters going to the zoo. Which of the following statements would work best?** (W.3.3.A)

    A. Zebras are located in the Africa section of the zoo.

    B. The zoo charges $12.50 for admission.

    C. I like going to the zoo with my class.

    D. Mary, Jim, and Tina arrived at the zoo in the afternoon.

18. **Which of the following sentences would work best when describing a character in a narrative?** (W.3.3.B)

    A. "Abby began to cry when she read the note..."

    B. "Digital cameras work best when..."

    C. "The American bald eagle has white feathers on its head..."

    D. "I think rabbits make better pets than hamsters because..."

=== **TRUE OR FALSE** ===

19. **You wrote a story about a man's experience climbing Mount Everest. At the end of the story, you wrote, "When it was all over, I looked back at the experience and was proud of myself for accomplishing my dream." This is an example of a narrative conclusion.** (W.3.3.D)

    A. True

    B. False

4. WRITING

WRITING PROMPT

20. **Write a narrative story about the last vacation you went on.** (W.3.3)

_____

_____

_____

_____

_____

_____

_____

_____

_____

_____

_____

_____

_____

_____

4.1. TEXT TYPES AND PURPOSE

4.2. PRODUCTION AND DISTRIBUTION OF WRITING

4. WRITING

~~ 4.2. Production and Distribution of Writing ~~

Common Core State Standard: CCSS.ELA-LITERACY.W.3.4, CCSS.ELA-LITERACY.W.3.5, CCSS.ELA-LITERACY.W.3.6

Skills:

- With guidance and support from adults, produce writing in which the development and organization are appropriate to task and purpose
- With guidance and support from peers and adults, develop and strengthen writing as needed by planning, revising, and editing
- With guidance and support from adults, use technology to produce and publish writing (using keyboarding skills) as well as to interact and collaborate with others

> ➤ **Directions:** *Read each writing prompt. Choose the sentence that would be the best opening sentence to answer each prompt.*

═══════ **EXAMPLE** ═══════

E1 You are running for class president. Write a speech that you will deliver in front of the student body. (W.3.4)

   A. As president, I will make sure that your voices are heard.

   B. How are you today?

   C. My favorite book has always been Charlotte's Web.

   D. Our current president is Donald Trump.

Answer: A. This sentence is the most appropriate way to address the task and purpose of your writing, which is to persuade students to vote for you.

4. WRITING

> **Directions:** *Read each sentence. Each one needs some editing. Rewrite each sentence in the space provided.*

=== **EXAMPLE** ===

E2   Mr. jones will be here at 9:00 (w.3.5)

_____

Answer: Mr. Jones will be here at 9:00. The "J" in Jones must be capitalized because it is a proper noun. Also, the sentence must end with a period, since it is a statement.

> **Directions:** *Read each task. Choose the computer program that would be best to complete the task.*

=== **EXAMPLE** ===

E3   Write a letter. (w.3.5)

   A. Microsoft Word   **B.** Microsoft PowerPoint
   C. The Internet   **D.** Email

Answer: **A.** Microsoft Word is a word processing program that is best used to create documents such as letters.

4. 2. PRODUCTION AND DISTRIBUTION OF WRITING

         prepaze

4. WRITING

> **Directions:** *Read each writing prompt. Choose the sentence that would be the BEST opening sentence to answer each prompt.*

=== **MULTIPLE CHOICE** ===

1. **You have just returned from a field trip to the children's museum. Write a letter thanking the museum curator for providing a tour, snacks, and a souvenir.** (W.3.4)

   A. What was your favorite part?

   B. The museum was so wonderful to explore.

   C. I loved the book that you shared with me.

   D. I am sorry that you could not attend.

2. **The newspaper is sponsoring a contest for Halloween. Write a short story about a time you were scared.** (W.3.4)

   A. It was a terrifying moment that I will never forget.

   B. It was the best moment of my life.

   C. Have you ever been so excited?

   D. The news was not what I expected.

3. **Your grandma sent you $100 in the mail for your birthday. Write a letter to her telling her how you plan to spend the money.** (W.3.4)

   A. The trip will be the best.

   B. The egg drop project is tomorrow.

   C. We will not have time to visit.

   D. You are the sweetest, most generous person ever.

4. **Recently the school cafeteria has stopped serving your favorite milk. Write a letter persuading them to start serving this milk again.** (W.3.4)

   A. Did you know students don't drink enough milk?

   B. I actually do not like milk.

   C. How are you today?

   D. What is for lunch?

4. WRITING

5. **Your best friend is traveling across the country for summer break. Write a letter telling him/her why you will miss them.** (W.3.4)

_____

_____

_____

_____

_____

_____

_____

_____

_____

_____

_____

_____

_____

_____

4.2. PRODUCTION AND DISTRIBUTION OF WRITING

 prepaze

4. WRITING

6. **Your puppy was recently treated at the local vet's office. Write a letter thanking the vet for taking care of the puppy.** (W.3.4)

_____

_____

_____

_____

_____

_____

_____

_____

_____

_____

_____

_____

_____

_____

_____

4.2. PRODUCTION AND DISTRIBUTION OF WRITING

4. WRITING

> **Directions:** *Read each sentence. Each one needs some editing. Rewrite each sentence in the space provided.*

═══════════ **FREE RESPONSE** ═══════════

7. **have you ever seen a fossil** (W.3.5)

_____

_____

_____

8. **last week, me and my family were on vacation.** (W.3.5)

_____

_____

_____

9. **i found a fossil inside a Rock.** (W.3.5)

_____

_____

_____

10. **It felt rough and different from the rest of the rock?** (W.3.5)

_____

_____

_____

4. 2. PRODUCTION AND DISTRIBUTION OF WRITING

4. WRITING

> **Directions:** *Look at each writing prompt. Complete the outline to plan your response.*

11. **Many people say that kids should eat more vegetables. Write about your favorite vegetables.** (W.3.5)

   I. I should eat vegetables because _____

   II. I like to eat _____ because _____

   II. I like to eat _____ because _____

   IV. I like to eat _____ because _____

12. **Have you ever read a book that you just couldn't put down? Write about one of those books.** (W.3.5)

   I. The book was called _____

   II. My favorite character was _____

   III. I was surprised because _____

   IV. I also liked _____

> **Directions:** *Read each set of sentences. Revise the sentences to get rid of the repeated words.*

13. **The dog is brown. The dog has a white nose. The dog has brown eyes.** (W.3.5)

   _____

   _____

   _____

   _____

   _____

   _____

4. WRITING

14. **My friend, Lily, will be here soon. My friend, Tessa, will be here soon. My friend, Becky, will be here soon.** (W.3.5)

_____

_____

_____

_____

_____

_____

> ➢ **Directions:** *Read each task. Choose the computer program that would be best to complete the task.*

═══════════ **MULTIPLE CHOICE** ═══════════

15. **Create a multimedia presentation.** (W.3.6)

    A. Microsoft Word **B.** Microsoft PowerPoint
    C. The Internet **D.** Email

16. **Complete research about snow leopards.** (W.3.6)

    A. Microsoft Word **B.** Microsoft PowerPoint
    C. The Internet **D.** Email

17. **Ask teacher a question about the upcoming project.** (W.3.6)

    A. Microsoft Word **B.** Microsoft PowerPoint
    C. The Internet **D.** Email

18. **Type a short story.** (W.3.6)

    A. Microsoft Word **B.** Microsoft PowerPoint
    C. The Internet **D.** Email

 prepaze

4. WRITING

=== **FREE RESPONSE** ===

19. **You want to search for oceans on the internet. Describes the steps that you would take in order to complete your search.** (W.3.6)

_____

_____

_____

_____

_____

20. **You want to change the color and size of the font (letter style) as you are typing a document in Microsoft Word. Describe the steps that you would take in order to complete this task.** (W.3.6)

_____

_____

_____

_____

_____

4.3. BUILD AND PRESENT KNOWLEDGE

4. WRITING

~~~ 4.3. Build and Present Knowledge ~~~

Common Core State Standards: CCSS.ELA-LITERACY.W.3.7, CCSS.ELA-LITERACY.W.3.8

Skills:

- Conduct short research projects that build knowledge about a topic
- Recall information from experiences or gather information from print and digital sources; take brief notes on sources and sort evidence into provided categories

> ➢ **Directions:** *Read each question. Choose the multiple choice answer that best answers each question.*

=== **EXAMPLE** ===

E1 **You are trying to find out the definition for 'omnipotent'. What resource should you use to complete the research?** (w.3.7)

  A. Dictionary   **B.** Thesaurus
  C. Encyclopedia   **D.** Textbook

Answer: **A.** A dictionary should be used to look up word definitions.

E2 **You are taking notes about bee colonies for a research paper. Which answer choice is the best way to sort your information?** (w.3.8)

  A. Write a one-page summary of all the info you collected.
  B. Create categories, such as queen bees and worker bees, and sort your info.
  C. Highlight key details in the book that you used for research.
  D. Create a long list of notes with all the info you collected.

Answer: **B.** Creating categories, such as queen bees and worker bees, is the best way to sort your info.

4. WRITING

> **Directions:** *Read each question. Choose the multiple choice answer that best answers each question.*

=== **MULTIPLE CHOICE** ===

1. **You are trying to find out when Harriet Tubman was born. What resource should you use to complete the research?** (W.3.7)

   A. Dictionary   **B.** Thesaurus   **C.** A map   **D.** The Internet

2. **You are trying to find out how the capital city of Texas. What resource should you use to complete the research?** (W.3.7)

   A. Dictionary   **B.** Thesaurus   **C.** A map   **D.** An almanac

3. **You are trying to find out who the sixteenth president of the United States was. What resource should you use to complete the research?** (W.3.7)

   A. Dictionary   **B.** Thesaurus   **C.** A map   **D.** The Internet

4. **You are trying to find out another word that means the same as 'big'. What resource should you use to complete the research?** (W.3.7)

   A. Dictionary   **B.** Thesaurus   **C.** Encyclopedia   **D.** Textbook

> **Directions:** *Read each sentence. Circle the keywords that would be used to complete research on the Internet related to the topic.* (W.3.7)

5. **George Washington was the first president of the United States.**

6. **The Siberian husky is a very interesting animal.**

7. **A Ferrari is an exotic sports car.**

4. WRITING

8. **The stalagmites and stalactites are beautiful inside the cave.**

9. **Cape Cod, Massachusetts is a beautiful vacation destination.**

10. **The seashells on Sanibel Island are incredible treasures.**

> ➢ **Directions:** *Look at the items listed in each category. Add a title for each category.* (W.3.8)

11.	12.	13.
Races/ Gives rides	Spins on wheels	Tallest mammal
Lives in a stable	Lives in a small cage	Lives in Africa
Needs to be brushed	Rodent	Eats tree leaves
Eats hay and grass	Eats vegetables	Tan with spots
Lives on a farm	Fat and furry	Can run up to 35 mph

4.3. BUILD AND PRESENT KNOWLEDGE

prepaze

4. WRITING

> **Directions:** *Look at each of the category titles. Sort the words from the word bank into the appropriate categories. Write each word from the word bank in the correct column.* (W.3.8)

Carrots	Beets	Roots	Apples	Pumpkins
Pears	Potatoes	Grapes	Tomatoes	Cucumbers
Oranges	Green beans	Peanuts	Bananas	Mangoes

4.3. BUILD AND PRESENT KNOWLEDGE

14. Grows on trees	15. Grows underground	16. Grows on vines

4. WRITING

> **Directions:** *Recall or look up information about two dog breeds. Compare and contrast, listing at least three similarities and three differences.* (W.3.8)

17. **Dog Breed #1**	**18.** **Dog Breed #2**
19. **Similarities**	**20.** **Differences**

4.3. BUILD AND PRESENT KNOWLEDGE

4.4. Range of Writing

4. WRITING

～～ 4.4. Range of Writing ～～

Common Core State Standards: CCSS.ELA-LITERACY.W.3.10

Skills:

- Write routinely over short and extended time frames

=== **EXAMPLE** ===

Kim is writing an essay about the inventor George Washington Carver. She read a biography about his accomplishments and took notes. Kim wants to start writing her essay, but she has too many notes and needs to organize them. She did not do well on the last assignment because her main idea was unclear. She also had too many unnecessary details in her essay. Kim really wants to get a good grade this time.

E1   **Which sentence best describes what Kim should do next?** (W.3.10)

- **A.** Kim should create an outline for her essay.
- **B.** Kim should start writing her essay.
- **C.** Kim should throw her notes away and start over.
- **D.** Kim should copy a few sentences from the biography.

Answer: **A.** Kim should create an outline for her essay. Outlines help to organize ideas before writing a text.

> ➤   **Directions:** *Li is revising the rough draft of her essay. Read the essay and answer the questions below.*

The San Diego Zoo is my favorite place to visit. I get to see many different animals all in one place! I can see monkeys, zebras, snakes and much more. Plus, I always learn new things about each animal. There are fun facts and helpful zoo guides with plenty of information. Whenever I want to have a fun adventure while learning about animals, I visit this zoo. **1** <u>San Diego is very hot in the summer</u>.

The San Diego Zoo has many different exhibits. Each one features animals from all over the world. My favorite exhibit is called the Northern Frontier.

...continued next page

4. WRITING

2 <u>There are pandas, foxes, and mountain lions in this area.</u> I once even saw a reindeer! That is the reason why I love this zoo. There is always an interesting variety of things to see. One time, my family and I took the Guided Bus Tour. **3** <u>This was great because we were able to see the exhibits as the announcer told us facts about the animals which was a lot of fun and my little brother loves buses.</u> We had so much fun that day.

4 <u>Did you know that a baby giraffe is called a calf.</u> This is one of the things that I learned at the San Diego Zoo. In fact, I learn something new every time I visit. I'm looking forward to going back so that I can learn much more. **5** <u>A fun and educational experience</u>.

MULTIPLE CHOICE

1. **Which sentence best describes how Li should revise sentence 1?** (W.3.10)

   A. Li should replace the word *very* with the word *extremely*.

   B. Li should not make any changes to this sentence.

   C. Li should not capitalize *San Diego*.

   D. Li should remove this sentence from the essay.

2. **Which sentence best demonstrates how Li can make sentence 2 more descriptive?** (W.3.10)

   A. There are many different animals in this area.

   B. There are cute pandas, fuzzy foxes, and ferocious mountain lions in this area.

   C. The are lots of pandas and many foxes and a huge amount of even more mountain lions.

   D. This sentence already uses descriptive language.

3. **Which statement best describes sentence 3?** (W.3.10)

   A. Sentence 3 is a run-on sentence.

   B. Sentence 3 is a fragment.

   C. Sentence 3 is the main idea of the paragraph.

   D. Sentence 3 contains no errors.

4.4. RANGE OF WRITING

prepaze

4. WRITING

4. **Which of the following is the best way to revise sentence 3?** (W.3.10)

A. This was great because we were able to see the exhibits as the announcer told us facts about the animals which was a lot of fun and my little brother loves buses.

B. This was great because we were able to see the exhibits. As the announcer told us facts about the animals, which was a lot of fun and my little brother loves buses.

C. This was great because we were able to see the exhibits as the announcer told us facts about the animals. My little brother, who loves buses, enjoyed the tour.

D. This was great because we were able. To see the exhibits as the announcer told us facts about the animals. Which was a lot of fun and my little brother loves buses.

5. **What is the error in sentence 4?** (W.3.10)

A. There is no error in sentence 4.

B. There should be a question mark at the end of the sentence.

C. There should be an exclamation point at the end of the sentence.

D. There are spelling errors in sentence 4.

6. **Which sentence best describes sentence 5?** (W.3.10)

A. Sentence 5 does not support the main idea.

B. Sentence 5 contains punctuation errors.

C. Sentence 5 is a fragment.

D. Sentence 5 should be removed from the essay.

7. **Which of the following is the best way to revise sentence 3?** (W.3.10)

A. The San Diego Zoo is a fun and educational experience.

B. A fun and educational experience.

C. A fun and educational experience?

D. The San Diego Zoo is a fun and educational experience and you should go because you're going to have so much fun because I do all the time.

4. WRITING

=== **WRITING PROMPT** ===

8. **Write a brief reflection essay about your favorite place to visit.** (W.3.10)

_____

_____

_____

_____

_____

_____

_____

_____

_____

_____

_____

_____

_____

_____

_____

_____

4.4. RANGE OF WRITING

prepaze

4. WRITING

> **Directions:** *Mr. Potter's science class has been observing plant growth for the past 5 weeks. Each week, the students sketched their observations and took notes in their journals. The students will now write a report about the project. Look at the information and answer the questions below.*

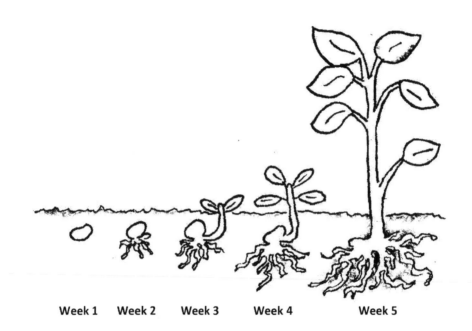

Week 1   Week 2   Week 3   Week 4   Week 5

Week 1	Week 2	Week 3	Week 4	Week 5
Today we planted a seed underground. I think it may take a few weeks to sprout.	I still do not see any changes in the seed. Our textbook says that the seed is still growing underground.	I saw a small sprout coming up from the ground today. I checked a website about plants. The website says that the sprout will become a seedling soon.	I measured the seedling today. It is now 5 inches tall.	The plant is now 2 feet tall! It has a thick stem and soft green leaves.

4. 4. RANGE OF WRITING

4. WRITING

═══════════════ **MULTIPLE CHOICE** ═══════════════

9. **Which sentence best describes the next step in writing the report?** (W.3.10)

   A. The students should take more notes.

   B. The students should use their notes to start developing an outline.

   C. The students should start writing their report.

   D. The students should start revising their rough draft.

10. **Which is the best example of a main idea for the report?** (W.3.10)

    A. The seed became a plant after 5 weeks of various changes.

    B. I saw a small sprout coming up from the ground today.

    C. We watered the plant daily.

    D. The seed was planted in a sunny spot outside.

11. **Which of the following sentences best supports the main idea?** (W.3.10)

    A. The students observed the plant for 5 weeks.

    B. A fern is an example of a houseplant.

    C. I measured the seedling today.

    D. At week 3, the seed started sprouting above the ground.

12. **Which is the best example of a concluding statement for this report?** (W.3.10)

    A. At week 4, the seedling was 5 inches tall.

    B. Finally, the seed had grown into a full plant.

    C. There were no changes observed during week 1.

    D. Seeds can grow into plants if they are properly cared for.

═══════════════ **TRUE OR FALSE** ═══════════════

13. **The students should start writing their reports during week 1.** (W.3.10)

    A. True   **B.** False

4. WRITING

14. **The students can use other resources, such as books, to write the report.** (W.3.10)

    A. True   **B.** False

15. **Observing and taking notes are part of the writing process.** (W.3.10)

    A. True   **B.** False

16. **The students do not have enough information to write the report.** (W.3.10)

    A. True   **B.** False

17. **Observation reports should never be revised.** (W.3.10)

    A. True   **B.** False

═══ WRITING PROMPT/FREE RESPONSE ═══

18. **Pretend that you are in Mr. Potter's science class. Write an introductory paragraph about your plant growth observation.** (W.3.10)

    _____

    _____

    _____

    _____

    _____

    _____

    _____

    _____

    _____

4. 4. RANGE OF WRITING

4. WRITING

19. **Explain how the students' research process is helpful for writing the report.** (W.3.10)

prepaze

4. WRITING

20. **Explain why Mr. Potter's project is an extended writing assignment.** (W.3.10)

_____

_____

_____

_____

_____

_____

_____

_____

_____

4. 4. RANGE OF WRITING

4.5. CHAPTER REVIEW

4. WRITING

~~~~~ 4.5. Chapter Review ~~~~~

> ➤ **Directions:** *Read the question and select the best answer choice.*

=== **MULTIPLE CHOICE** ===

1. **Read the response and select the appropriate writing prompt.** (W.3.4)

I know that you think dogs are a lot of work. I know they are, but I will help. I can take the dog for walks. I can also help with feeding it, brushing it, and giving it baths. I know it will take some work from you too, but I promise to do my part. Can we please get a puppy?

A. Write about a time when you were surprised.
B. Write about a time when you were trying to convince your parents to do something.
C. Write about something that you are good at.
D. Write about a time when you were sorry for making a mistake.

2. **Read each writing prompt. Choose the sentence that would be the best opening sentence to answer each prompt.** (W.3.4)

As part of the science fair, you have to write an article about your display. Write an article that informs about the chemical reaction you are displaying.

A. The combination of lemon juice and baking soda is powerful.
B. Do you like science?
C. I don't understand how to make science projects.
D. Let me ask you a question.

prepaze

4. WRITING

WRITING PROMPT

3. **Your school is choosing people to edit the school newspaper. Write a letter persuading the editor to choose you.** (W.3.4)

_____

_____

_____

_____

_____

_____

_____

_____

_____

_____

_____

_____

_____

4. WRITING

> **Directions:** *Read the question and select the best answer choice.*

═══════════════ **MULTIPLE CHOICE** ═══════════════

4. **You are trying to find out the definition for 'mediocre'. What resource should you use to complete the research?** (w.3.7)

    A. Dictionary   **B.** Thesaurus   **C.** Encyclopedia   **D.** A map

5. **You are trying to find out how far Ohio is from California. Which resource should you use?** (w.3.7)

    A. A map   **B.** An email   **C.** Encyclopedia   **D.** A blog

6. **Read the sentence. Circle the keywords that would be used to complete Internet research on the topic.** (w.3.7)

    Thomas Kinkade is a famous artist who has created artwork of lighthouses.

═══════════════ **FREE RESPONSE** ═══════════════

7. **Read the sentence. It needs some editing. Rewrite the sentence in the space provided.** (w.3.5)

    he has traveled all over arizona new mexico and utah

    _____

    _____

8. **Read the sentence. Revise in order to get rid of the repeated words.** (w.3.5)

    I bought grapes at the store. I bought bread at the store. I bought milk at the store.

    _____

    _____

       prepaze

4.5. CHAPTER REVIEW

4. WRITING

9. **Look at the writing prompt. Complete the outline to plan your response.** (W.3.5)

Some animals make better pets than others. Write an article about your favorite pet.

I. My favorite pet is _____

II. It's my favorite because _____

III. I also like it because _____

IV. It's the best pet because _____

10. **You want to copy and paste text as you are creating a document in Microsoft Word. Describe the steps that you would take in order to complete this task.** (W.3.6)

_____

_____

_____

_____

_____

_____

_____

_____

_____

_____

_____

4. WRITING

MULTIPLE CHOICE

11. **Read the task. Choose the computer program that would be best to complete the task.** (W.3.6)

Send a message to a friend in another country.

A. Microsoft Word
B. Microsoft PowerPoint
C. The Internet
D. Email

12. **Your teacher asks you to write about the best vacation you ever went on. You will be writing a(n):** (W.3.1)

A. Informative text
B. Research paper
C. Narrative piece
D. Opinion piece

13. **If you are writing about why people should wear seatbelts, which of the following statements would be a good reason to use as support?** (W.3.1.A, W.3.1.B)

A. Seatbelts can break over time.

B. Seatbelts save about 50% of passengers who wear them from being seriously hurt.

C. Seatbelts come in different colors and buckle styles.

D. Seatbelts can latch across your waist.

14. **Which of the following is a linking word or phrase?** (W.3.1.C)

A. Because
B. For example
C. In the meantime
D. All of the above

15. **Your teacher asks you to write about how dolphins communicate. You will be writing an:** (W.3.2)

A. A. Informative text
B. Group paper
C. Narrative piece
D. Opinion piece

16. **Which of the following is not a linking word or phrase?** (W.3.2.C)

A. Who
B. Another
C. More
D. Also

prepaze

4. WRITING

TRUE OR FALSE

17. **When writing an informative text, you should include characters and dialogue.** (W.3.2.A, W.3.2.B)

    A. True   **B.** False

18. **You wrote a paper about how a factory makes crayons. At the beginning of the paper, you write, "Crayons start from wax and eventually become the coloring sticks that we use every day." This is an example of an introductory statement.** (W.3.2.A, W.3.2.D)

    A. True   **B.** False

19. **If you were writing facts about Martin Luther King, Jr., you would be writing a narrative.** (W.3.3)

    A. True   **B.** False

20. **Narratives use dialogue and descriptions to show how characters respond to situations.** (W.3.3.B)

    A. True   **B.** False

21. **You wrote the statement, "Before Molly could run the race, she first had to practice running on the school track." The words "before" and "first" are examples of temporal words that signal event order.** (W.3.3.C)

    A. True   **B.** False

4. WRITING

22. **Write a narrative about a character going on a camping trip. Make sure to introduce and develop the characters, and provide a sense of closure.** (W.3.3)

_____

_____

_____

_____

_____

_____

_____

_____

_____

_____

_____

_____

_____

_____

_____

4.5. CHAPTER REVIEW

prepaze

4. WRITING

> **Directions:** Look at each of the category titles. Sort the words from the word bank into the appropriate categories. Write each word from the word bank in the correct column.
> (W.3.8)

Salt water	Jellyfish	Scorpions	Bears	Seashells
Cactus	Deep sea fishing	Mountain Lions	Squirrels	Rabbits
Whales	Camels	Tall trees	Sandstorms	Sand

23. Desert	24. Ocean	25. Mountains

4. WRITING

26. Pretend that you are writing a research paper about animal habitats. Explain how you would use the table to take notes for your planning. (W.3.8)

_____

_____

_____

_____

_____

_____

_____

> ➤ **Directions:** _Joshua has one week to complete an essay. Each day, he will complete part of the writing process in class. Read his teacher's instructions and answer the questions below._

MRS. JOHNSON'S CLASS

American History Essay

Assignment details: You will select an important moment in American history and write an essay about the topic. The weekly writing schedule is as follows:

Day 1: Research your topic

Day 2: Create an outline of your paper

Day 3: Write a rough draft of your report

Day 4: Revise your report

Day 5: Final edits/submit a final draft

prepaze

4. WRITING

=== **MULTIPLE CHOICE** ===

27. Which sentence best describes how Joshua should begin the writing process? (W.3.10)

  A. Joshua should start writing his essay as soon as possible.

  B. Joshua should start making revisions to his essay.

  C. Joshua should start researching his topic.

  D. Joshua should start creating an outline.

28. Which of the following resources should Joshua use first? (W.3.10)

  A. An American history book

  B. A dictionary

  C. A thesaurus

  D. A website about essay writing tips

29. Which answer best describes how Joshua's outline should be organized? (W.3.10)

  A. Topic, supporting details, the main idea

  B. Topic, main idea, introduction, supporting details, conclusion

  C. Introduction and conclusion

  D. Topic, summary, conclusion

30. Which answer best describes the meaning of *rough draft*? (W.3.10)

  A. A rough draft is the final version of an essay.

  B. A rough draft is the first version of an essay.

  C. A rough draft is a list of research notes.

  D. A rough draft is a revised version of an essay.

4.5. CHAPTER REVIEW

5. LANGUAGE

5. LANGUAGE

~~~ 5.1. Conventions of Standard English ~~~

Common Core State Standards: CCSS.ELA-LITERACY.L.3.1, CCSS.ELA-LITERACY.L.3.2

Skills:
- Demonstrate command of the conventions of standard English grammar and usage when writing or speaking
- Demonstrate command of the conventions of standard English capitalization, punctuation, and spelling when writing

=== **EXAMPLE QUESTION** ===

➢ **Directions:** *Complete the sentence below with the correct <u>collective noun</u>.*

E1   Ms. Smith quickly collected the tests after the bell rang. (L.3.1)

   A. Noun   **B.** Verb   **C.** Adjective   **D.** Adverb

Correct Answer: D. The word quickly is an adverb because it describes the verb collected.

E2   My favorite book to read is *Charlie and the Chocolate Factory*. (L.3.2)

   A. Favorite   **B.** Book   **C.** Read   **D.** Charlie

Correct Answer: D. The word Charlie needs to be capitalized because it is a proper name and is the first word in a book title.

=== **MULTIPLE CHOICE** ===

➢ **Directions:** *Read the sentences. Identify the part of speech that is underlined.*

1.   My family went to a tropical <u>island</u> for vacation. (L.3.1)

   A. Noun   **B.** Pronoun   **C.** Adjective   **D.** Verb

5. LANGUAGE

2. **My brother <u>drove</u> me to school today in his new car.** (L.3.1)

    A. Noun   **B.** Adverb   **C.** Adjective   **D.** Verb

3. **I cannot believe <u>they</u> got to go to the concert last weekend.** (L.3.1)

    A. Noun   **B.** Pronoun   **C.** Adjective   **D.** Adverb

> **Directions:** *Read the passage. Then answer the questions that follow.*

> Deep in the woods there were many animals. Among the trees there was a <u>deer</u>. A brown <u>fox</u> jumped over a nearby log and ran out of sight. In the distance, there was a large <u>ox</u> standing in an open field.

4. **Change the singular noun <u>deer</u> to a plural noun.** (L.3.1)

    A. Deer   **B.** Deers   **C.** Deeres   **D.** Deerss

5. **Change the singular noun <u>fox</u> to a plural noun.** (L.3.1)

    A. Fox   **B.** Foxs   **C.** Foxes   **D.** Foxss

6. **Change the singular noun <u>ox</u> to a plural noun.** (L.3.1)

    A. Ox   **B.** Oxs   **C.** Oxes   **D.** Oxen

> **Directions:** *Read the sentences. Identify the abstract noun.*

7. **It will take a lot of strength to lift that car.** (L.3.1)

    A. Take   **B.** Strength   **C.** Lift   **D.** Car

> **Directions:** *Read the sentences. Identify the correct possessive form of the nouns below.*

8. **Where is _____ computer?** (L.3.2)

    A. Katie   **B.** Katie's   **C.** Katies   **D.** Katies'

5. LANGUAGE

9. Our _____ vacation house is in Florida. (L.3.2)

   A. family   **B.** family's   **C.** families   **D.** families'

10. The _____ helmets were in the fire truck. (L.3.2)

    A. firefighter   **B.** firefighter's   **C.** firefighters   **D.** firefighters'

> **Directions:** *Read the sentences with the underlined base word below. Circle the word that is not spelled correctly.*

11. **Please <u>sit</u> quietly at your desks.** (L.3.2)

    A. Sits   **B.** Sitting   **C.** Sitted   **D.** Sat

12. **You have a very pretty <u>smile</u>.** (L.3.2)

    A. Smiles   **B.** Smiled   **C.** Smiling   **D.** Smilling

13. **Please don't <u>cry</u> over what happened yesterday.** (L.3.2)

    A. Cries   **B.** Crying   **C.** Cried   **D.** Crys

14. **I am so <u>happy</u> to see you accomplish your dream.** (L.3.2)

    A. Happier   **B.** Happiest   **C.** Happyness   **D.** Happiness

> **Directions:** *Read each passage. Answer the questions that follow.*

The police officer stopped along the side of the busy street. He saw something that looked suspicious. He used the radio inside the police car to contact the police station. He put on his hat and made sure that his _____ was visible.

15. **Which is the correct spelling for the missing word in the passage?** (L.3.2)

    A. Bag   **B.** Bage   **C.** Badge   **D.** Badg

5. LANGUAGE

=== **FREE RESPONSE** ===

> **Directions:** *Read each passage. Then combine the last two underlined sentences into one sentence using the correct coordinating conjunction (and, but, for, nor, or, so, yet).*

16. **I really struggled with history class. I was not very good at memorizing names and dates so the subject was hard for me to learn. On Monday, our teacher assigned us history homework. <u>My homework was difficult. It took me a long time to complete.</u>** (L.3.1)

_____

_____

_____

_____

17. **I went to the pond with my little sister. She loved to feed the ducks and to see all of the animals nearby. She asked me to pick up a frog for her so she could see it up close. I reached down and picked up a tiny green frog. <u>The frog was really slippery. It jumped out of my hand.</u>** (L.3.1)

_____

_____

_____

_____

5.1. CONVENTIONS OF STANDARD ENGLISH

prepaze

5. LANGUAGE

> ➢ **Directions:** *Read each passage. Then combine the last two under-lined sentences into one sentence using the correct sub-ordinating conjunction (after, although, because, before, if, once, since).*

18. I began to see very strange things. I saw a big, dark cloud of smoke coming from downstairs. "What was going on?" I thought. I wanted to run out of the house, but I couldn't move my feet. <u>I woke up scared. I had a nightmare.</u> (L.3.1)

_____

_____

_____

_____

_____

19. When the school bell rang, Katie packed up her schoolbag in a hurry. She wanted to get home before it started to rain. Katie ran out the school doors and headed toward her house. <u>She walked home from school. She realized her mom was picking her up.</u> (L.3.1)

_____

_____

_____

_____

_____

5. LANGUAGE

> ➤ **Directions:** *Read each passage. Place <u>commas</u> and <u>quotation marks</u> where needed in the sentences below.*

20. I was so tired after a long day playing baseball in the hot weather. My sister whispered Are you asleep? Yes, I was I responded in anger. Sorry, I didn't know you were that tired she said. The room was quiet again. I quickly fell back into a deep sleep. (L.3.2)

5.2. KNOWLEDGE OF LANGUAGE

prepaze

5. LANGUAGE

~~~ 5.2. Knowledge of Language ~~~

Common Core State Standard: CCSS.ELA-LITERACY.L.3.3

Skill: *Use knowledge of language and its conventions when writing, speaking, reading, or listening.*

- Choose words and phrases for effect.
- Recognize and observe differences between the conventions of spoken and written standard English.

═══════ **EXAMPLE** ═══════

> **Directions:** *Read the sentence below. Identify which phrase adds effect.*

E1 The ocean waves were crashing violently against the rocks. (L.3.3)

   A. ocean waves   **B.** crashing violently
   C. against the rocks   **D.** were crashing

Correct Answer: B. The phrase "crashing violently" adds an effect or creates a picture in the mind of the reader. It describes what the waves looked like when they hit against the rocks.

═══════ **MULTIPLE CHOICE** ═══════

> **Directions:** *Read the sentences below. Identify which words or phrases add effect. Choose the best answer.*

1. **The young puppy ran around the backyard creating a dizzy-looking figure eight.** (L.3.3)

   A. young puppy   **B.** ran around
   C. backyard creating   **D.** dizzy-looking figure eight

5. 2. KNOWLEDGE OF LANGUAGE

prepaze   **www.prepaze.com**

5. LANGUAGE

2. **The slippery tadpole made its way through the pond.** (L.3.3)

   A. slippery   **B.** tadpole   **C.** way   **D.** pond

3. **When he won the race, he leaped like a frog in the air.** (L.3.3)

   A. won   **B.** won the race
   C. leaped   **D.** leaped like a frog

4. **After the heavy snowstorm hit the town, the ground looked like it was covered in shiny diamonds.** (L.3.3)

   A. heavy snowstorm   **B.** hit the town
   C. the ground   **D.** covered in shiny diamonds

5. **The field of yellow daisies danced in the twirling wind.** (L.3.3)

   A. yellow daisies   **B.** field of yellow daisies
   C. danced   **D.** danced in the twirling wind

6. **The playful dolphins swam behind the ship.** (L.3.3)

   A. playful   **B.** dolphins
   C. swam   **D.** ship

7. **The boiling kettle let out a shrieking scream on the stove.** (L.3.3)

   A. boiling   **B.** kettle
   C. shrieking scream   **D.** stove

> **Directions:** *Read each passage. Answer the questions that follow.*

The teacher was excited to see her new students on the first day of school. She had decorated the room so that the students would enjoy their beautiful surroundings. The teacher stocked the room with brand new supplies to last for the entire school year. The teacher had a bright, shiny smile that lit up her face.

8. **Which of the phrases below adds effect to the passage? Choose the best answer.** (L.3.3)

   A. decorated the room   **B.** beautiful surroundings
   C. brand new supplies   **D.** a bright, shiny smile that lit up her face

 prepaze

5. LANGUAGE

Ms. Franklin had a pair of rabbits that were tearing up her flowers. Every morning she would see the rabbits digging in her garden. Ms. Franklin would tap on the window, and the rabbits would quickly shoot up their pointy ears and freeze. The rabbits would stop digging and look at each other. The pair would hop away until they were out of sight.

9. **Which of the phrases below adds effect to the passage? Choose the best answer.** (L.3.3)

   A. tearing up her flowers
   B. digging in her garden
   C. quickly shoot up their pointy ears and freeze
   D. hop away

The hometown team was ready to play. The athletes were hungry for a victory. The players sat in the middle of the cold gym floor and stretched their legs. They practiced doing layup drills and passing the basketball. The team captain pulled the team in to go over the first play of the game they planned to run.

10. **Which of the phrases below adds effect to the passage? Choose the best answer.** (L.3.3)

   A. hometown team   **B.** hungry for a victory
   C. cold gym floor   **D.** team captain

The bald eagle spotted its prey in the lake below. It was hungry and wanted to eat the fish. The eagle dove straight down toward the lake. It quickly glided above the crystal blue water to grab its prey. The eagle caught the fish with its claws. It flew back up into the sky with the fish.

11. **Which of the phrases below adds effect to the passage? Choose the best answer.** (L.3.3)

   A. spotted its prey
   B. dove straight down toward the lake
   C. quickly glided above the crystal blue water
   D. caught the fish with its claws

5. LANGUAGE

The group of friends decided they wanted to go ice skating during winter break. They stood in line and rented pairs of ice skates. The friends laced up their skates and were ready to head onto the ice. The friends began to slip and slide up and down the ice rink. They looked shaky on their feet.

12. **Which of the phrases below adds effect to the passage? Choose the best answer.** (L.3.3)

   A. rented pairs of ice skates

   B. laced up their skates

   C. slip and slide up and down the ice rink

   D. looked shaky on their feet

TRUE OR FALSE

> **Directions:** *Mark the following statements as either true or false.*

13. **Read the sentence: "Thank you, sir." This sentence is formal English.** (L.3.3)

   A. True   **B.** False

14. **Read the sentence: "Dude, that was some party!" This sentence is informal English.** (L.3.3)

   A. True   **B.** False

15. **Read the sentence: "How are you?" This sentence is informal English.** (L.3.3)

   A. True   **B.** False

16. **Read the sentence: "Can you help me, please?" This sentence is formal English.** (L.3.3)

   A. True   **B.** False

17. **Read the sentence: "LOL! That was so cool!" This sentence is informal English.** (L.3.3)

   A. True   **B.** False

5.2. KNOWLEDGE OF LANGUAGE

5. LANGUAGE

18. **Read the sentence: "What are we having for dinner tonight?" This sentence is informal English.** (L.3.3)

    A. True   **B.** False

19. **Read the passage: The mom took her young daughter to the local park. She watched as her little girl played on the swing set and ran quickly up the slide. "Please be careful!" cried the mom. The young girl looked over to where her mom was standing and smiled.**

    This passage is written in formal English. (L.3.3)

    A. True   **B.** False

20. **Read the passage: "Oh my gosh, did you guys see that? No, look over there behind that big, weird-looking thing. It totally looks like a giant monster to me. I don't know. Maybe I'm wrong, but it really scared me when I first looked at it."**

    This passage is spoken in informal English. (L.3.3)

    A. True   **B.** False

5.3. VOCABULARY ACQUISITION AND USE

5. LANGUAGE

~~~ 5.3. Vocabulary Acquisition and Use ~~~

Common Core State Standards: CCSS.ELA-LITERACY.L.3.4, CCSS.ELA-LITERACY.L.3.5, CCSS.ELA-LITERACY.L.3.6

Skills:

- Determine or clarify the meaning of unknown and multiple-meaning word and phrases based on grade 3 reading and content, choosing flexibly from a range of strategies.
- Demonstrate understanding of figurative language, word relationships and nuances in word meanings.
- Acquire and use accurately grade-appropriate conversational, general academic, and domain-specific words and phrases, including those that signal spatial and temporal relationships (e.g., *After dinner that night we went looking for them*).

═══════════ **EXAMPLE** ═══════════

> ➤ *Directions: Read the passage and answer the questions.*

She leaned back in her beach chair. The blue ocean stretched out in front of her. It seemed to go on and on forever. The waves made a soothing sound as they lapped against the shore.

Jessica opened her cooler bag. She took out a peanut butter sandwich and a bottle of water. As soon as she unwrapped the sandwich a seagull flew in. It stared at her sandwich. Jessica laughed.

E1   What does the word lapped refer to in this passage? (L.3.4)

- **A.** pass someone in a race
- **B.** overlap two things
- **C.** Drinking with your tongue
- **D.** How the ocean waves hit the beach

Answer: D. The word lapped is describing how the waves are hitting the beach.

5.3. VOCABULARY ACQUISITION AND USE

5. LANGUAGE

> ➤ *Directions: Read the passage and answer the questions.*

She leaned back in her beach chair. The blue ocean stretched out in front of her. It seemed to go on and on forever. The waves made a soothing sound as they lapped against the shore.

Jessica opened her cooler bag. She took out a peanut butter sandwich and a bottle of water. As soon as she unwrapped the sandwich a seagull flew in. It stared at her sandwich. Jessica laughed.

E2   **The excerpt above is most likely from a** (L.3.5)

A. Poem   **B.** Novel   **C.** Riddle   **D.** play

Answer: **B.** The excerpt is most likely from a novel.

> ➤ *Directions: Read the passage and answer the questions.*

She leaned back in her beach chair. The blue ocean stretched out in front of her. It seemed to go on and on forever. The waves made a soothing sound as they lapped against the shore.

Jessica opened her cooler bag. She took out a peanut butter sandwich and a bottle of water. As soon as she unwrapped the sandwich a seagull flew in. It stared at her sandwich. Jessica laughed.

E3   **This story is being told by** (L.3.6)

A. Jessica   **B.** A Seagull
C. Jessica's brother   **D.** Narrator

Answer: **D.** This story is being told by a narrator.

5. LANGUAGE

> ➤ *Directions: Read the passage and answer the questions.*

THE FOX AND THE CROW

One bright morning as the Fox was following his sharp nose through the wood in search of a bite to eat, he saw a Crow on the limb of a tree overhead. This was by no means the first Crow the Fox had ever seen. What caught his attention this time and made him stop for a second look, was that the lucky Crow held a bit of cheese in her beak.

"No need to search any farther," thought sly Master Fox. "Here is a dainty bite for my breakfast."

Up he trotted to the foot of the tree in which the Crow was sitting, and looking up admiringly, he cried, "Good-morning, beautiful creature!"

The Crow, her head cocked on one side, watched the Fox suspiciously. But she kept her beak tightly closed on the cheese and did not return his greeting.

"What a charming creature she is!" said the Fox. "How her feathers shine! What a beautiful form and what splendid wings! Such a wonderful Bird should have a very lovely voice, since everything else about her is so perfect. Could she sing just one song, I know I should hail her Queen of Birds."

Listening to these flattering words, the Crow forgot all her suspicion, and also her breakfast. She wanted very much to be called Queen of Birds. So she opened her beak wide to utter her loudest caw, and down fell the cheese straight into the Fox's open mouth.

"Thank you," said Master Fox sweetly, as he walked off. "Though it is cracked, you have a voice sure enough. But where are your wits?"

prepaze

5. LANGUAGE

1. **What does the Fox mean when he says, "I should hail her Queen of Birds."?** (L.3.4)

   _____

   _____

   _____

   _____

   _____

2. **What does the phrase, "sly Master Fox" tell the reader?** (L.3.4)

   _____

   _____

   _____

   _____

   _____

3. **What is the fox saying when he says, "Though it is cracked, you have a voice sure enough."** (L.3.4)

   _____

   _____

   _____

5.3. VOCABULARY ACQUISITION AND USE

5. LANGUAGE

_____

_____

_____

=== TRUE OR FALSE ===

4. **The Birds voice is broken.** (L.3.4)

   A. True   **B.** False

5. **If the bird has a beautiful voice she can become queen of all of the birds.** (L.3.4)

   A. True   **B.** False

> ➤ _Directions: Read the passage and answer the questions._

THE FABLE OF THE LION AND THE HARE

In ancient times, a ferocious lion lived in the forest, killing without remorse. The other animals were terrified. To stop the lion's deadly hunts, some animals offered to provide him with food each day. Some animals would still die, of course, but the rest would live in peace. The lion agreed and enjoyed months of the easy life. One day it was the hare's turn to present himself to the lion. Although small, the hare was very crafty.

"Lion, lion," the hare cried out as he approached. "Help me, help me! Another lion is trying to eat me. But I am to be your dinner! You must stop him!"

Furious that another lion was trying to steal his food, the lion demanded, "Take me to the thief. I will make him pay for this mischief!"

The hare and the lion made their way through the forest, eventually reaching the deep well. There the lion looked down and saw his own reflection in the water. Thinking he had found the creature who tried to steal his food, the lion jumped down, ready to fight. Alas, the lion never came out of that well, and the animals lived in peace from that day on.

     prepaze

VOCABULARY ACQUISITION AND USE · **5. 3.**

=== **FREE RESPONSE** ===

6. **What does it mean that the hare is "crafty"?** (L.3.4)

_____

_____

_____

_____

_____

=== **FILL IN THE BLANK** ===

7. **Another word for furious is** _____. (L.3.4)

=== **MULTIPLE CHOICE** ===

8. **"I will make him pay for <u>this mischief</u>!"**

Which phrase could replace the underlined phrase? (L.3.4)

A. being in the forest B. not listening
C. Taking my food D. talking to my animals

➢ _Directions: Read the passage and answer the questions._

AFTERNOON ON A HILL

I will be the gladdest thing
Under the sun!
I will touch a hundred flowers
And not pick one.

...continued next page

prepaze　　Copyrighted Material　　**www.prepaze.com**

5. LANGUAGE

I will look at cliffs and clouds
With quiet eyes,
Watch the wind bow down the grass,
And the grass rise.

And when lights begin to show
Up from the town,
I will mark which must be mine,
And then start down!

=== **FREE RESPONSE** ===

9. **Why do you think the author started this piece with the line "I will be the gladdest thing?"** (L.3.5)

_____

_____

_____

_____

_____

_____

10. **What genre is this work? How do you know?** (L.3.5)

_____

_____

_____

_____

prepaze

5. LANGUAGE

_____

_____

11. **Why did the author put a line break between lines three and four?** (L.3.5)

_____

_____

_____

_____

_____

_____

5.3. VOCABULARY ACQUISITION AND USE

=== **FILL IN THE BLANK** ===

12. **Each stanza of a poem is made of up** _____. (L.3.5)

13. **This poem has** _____ **stanzas.** (L.3.5)

> ➤ *Directions: Read the passage and answer the questions.*

Out West

Eliza stared out of the back of the covered wagon. Fields of grass stretched for miles and miles behind them. Eliza thought she had felt every single bump of the wagon along the way.

Riding in the back of the wagon was definitely not comfortable. She and her sister Martha were squeezed in among all of the family's belongings. Wooden chests held clothes and blankets. Crates held her mother's iron pots and pans. A barrel held bread and dried meat for the long journey.

...continued next page

   www.prepaze.com

5. LANGUAGE

Eliza sighed. She had been happy at their home in Ohio. But her father was eager to settle out west. There was rich farmland for the taking out there. He dreamed of a cabin and fields of corn. But Eliza missed her little house in Ohio. She missed her friends. She knew life on a farm was hard work. Would there even be a school out there?

Her father didn't seem to care about these things. "The Civil War is over," he said. "It's time for a fresh start for all of us." So they had packed up their belongings and joined the next wagon train out west.

Eliza was relieved when the wagon came to a stop. The wagons in the train formed a circle. It was time to get out, stretch, and cook the evening meal. The men had killed some wild pheasants the day before, so dinner would be tasty, at least.

Eliza hopped out of the wagon. They were in the middle of a prairie. Colorful flowers grew among the tall grasses. They made Eliza smile. She still wasn't happy about the move out west. But at least the flowers were pretty.

=== **FILL IN THE BLANK** ===

14. **This story is broken up into groups of sentences called** _____ . (L.3.5)

15. **The people in the story are the** _____ . (L.3.5)

=== **MULTIPLE CHOICE** ===

16. **This type of writing is called a** (L.3.5)

A. Play   **B.** Poem   **C.** Story   **D.** script

> ➤ *Directions: Read the passage and answer the questions.*

THE WISE CHOICE

"You have rescued my horse," Queen Olivia told the young boy standing before her. "Now you shall have a reward." Peter nervously ran his fingers through his brown hair. The frightened horse had run

...continued next page

past him as he worked in the field that morning. He would have helped it whether it belonged to the queen or not. But he had to admit that getting a reward was nice.

Two of the queen's pages appeared. One carried a small pillow with a mirror sitting on top. Red jewels sparkled on top of the mirror's silver frame. The other page carried a wood cage with a clucking chicken inside it.

"Only one reward can be yours," the queen said. "Choose wisely." "That's easy," Peter said. "I'll take the chicken." Some of the people in the court laughed. It was clear they thought he had made a foolish choice.

"And why did you choose the chicken?" the queen asked. "Well, I don't know much about jewels and things," Peter answered. "But I do know about chickens. The chicken will provide eggs for my family for a long while."

Queen Olivia smiled. "Then you did make a wise choice," she said. "That mirror may look fancy. But the jewels you see are only colored glass, and the frame is painted silver. The chicken is much more valuable." Peter took the chicken from the page. Then he bowed. "Thank you, your majesty."

"You are a smart child," the queen said. "I could use a smart boy to help take care of my horses. Would you like a job?" Peter grinned. "Thank you!" he said. A job at the castle paid well. Now his family would eat well for the rest of their lives—all because he had chosen a chicken!

=== **FREE RESPONSE** ===

17. What perspective is this story written from? How do you know? (L.3.6)

_____

_____

_____

_____

_____

5. LANGUAGE

18. **Does a job at the castle pay well? How do you know?** (L.3.6)

_____

_____

_____

_____

_____

19. **Do you agree or disagree with the Queen that Peter made a wise choice? Why?** (L.3.6)

_____

_____

_____

_____

_____

=== **FILL IN THE BLANK** ===

20. **Which character felt nervous?** _____ (L.3.6)

5.4. CHAPTER REVIEW

prepaze

5. LANGUAGE

~~~~~ 5.4. Chapter Review ~~~~~

> **Directions:** *Read the sentences. Identify the part of speech that is underlined.*

1. **The phrase "I walked" is what verb tense of the verb walk?** (L.3.1)
   - **A.** Past Tense
   - **B.** Present Tense
   - **C.** Future Tense
   - **D.** Special Tense

2. **The phrase "I walk" is what verb tense of the verb walk?** (L.3.1)
   - **A.** Past Tense
   - **B.** Present Tense
   - **C.** Future Tense
   - **D.** Special Tense

3. **The phrase "I will walk" is what verb tense of the verb walk?** (L.3.1)
   - **A.** Past Tense
   - **B.** Present Tense
   - **C.** Future Tense
   - **D.** Special Tense

> **Directions:** *Select the meaning of the word.*

4. **What does the word <u>churn</u> mean in the following sentence?** (L.3.2)

   Then the water around them began to <u>churn</u>.
   - **A.** Move
   - **B.** Swirl
   - **C.** Push
   - **D.** Run

> **Directions:** *Reach each passage. Answer the questions that follow.*

   Peter was training for a marathon. He found a flat trail to run on every morning. He needed to make sure he ran at least ten miles each day so that he would be conditioned for the race. After a few weeks, Peter increased the _____ he ran.

5. **Which is the correct spelling for the missing word in the passage?** (L.3.2)
   - **A.** Distence
   - **B.** Distance
   - **C.** Destence
   - **D.** Destance

5. LANGUAGE

Jerry and Julie wanted to do something exciting to celebrate their anniversary. They decided that they should take a hot air _____ ride up in the sky. When they were floating in the air, they looked down on their town. They could see the tops of trees and buildings. It was thrilling for them to see the skyline from this position.

6. **Which is the correct spelling for the missing word in the passage?** (L.3.2)

   A. Balloon   **B.** Baloon   **C.** Ballon   **D.** Balloun

Ms. Thomas made a feast for her family for the holidays. She had so much trash that she had to have the trash can _____ every few hours. Between all of the paper plates, napkins, and package wrappings, there was a lot of trash to throw away by the end of the meal.

7. **Which is the correct spelling for the missing word in the passage?** (L.3.2)

   A. Emptyed   **B.** Emptied   **C.** Emptyd   **D.** Emptid

The group of friends decided they wanted to go ice skating during winter break. They stood in line and rented pairs of ice skates. The friends laced up their skates and were ready to head onto the ice. The friends began to slip and slide up and down the ice rink. They looked shaky on their feet.

8. **Which of the phrases below adds effect to the passage? Choose the best answer.** (L.3.3)

   A. spotted its prey
   B. dove straight down toward the lake
   C. quickly glided above the crystal blue water
   D. caught the fish with its claws

The hometown team was ready to play. The athletes were hungry for a victory. The players sat in the middle of the cold gym floor and stretched their legs. They practiced doing layup drills and passing the basketball. The team captain pulled the team in to go over the first play of the game they planned to run.

prepaze

5. LANGUAGE

9. **Which of the phrases below adds effect to the passage? Choose the best answer.** (L.3.3)

    A. rented pairs of ice skates

    B. laced up their skates

    C. slip and slide up and down the ice rink

    D. looked shaky on their feet

> Please calm down, dear. I know everything will work out just fine. See, the weather is changing already. Soon we will be able to go back outside and look for your missing necklace. I am confident that we will find it somewhere in the backyard.

10. **This passage is spoken in informal English.** (L.3.3)

    A. True   **B.** False

> ➤ **Directions:** *Read the passage and answer the questions.*

THE NOISIEST CAT

At night, Roger would sit outside her door perched like a hen on an egg. All night long, Roger would wait for Melissa to wake up. At first, he would wait quietly. But after a few hours, he would start to get impatient. Every night, at around one in the morning, Roger would start to yowl.

If you do not have a cat, you do not know what an awful noise a yowl can be. Cats make lots of nice noises—like purring and meowing and sneezing—but a yowl is not nice at all. It starts deep inside their throat and moves up slowly, getting louder all the time. "Heeeeeee-yowl!" Roger would say, over and over again. It sounded like he was being stepped on. It sounded like he was in pain. And it woke Melissa up every time. Her eyes would pop open. Her stomach would twist up. She would lie there for hours, listening to Roger's awful cry. No human is strong enough to sleep through a yowling cat.

"Mom!" Melissa would say the next day. "Roger was yowling again last night. He kept me up for hours!"

"Oh sweetie," Mom would say. "He just can't stand to be without you. He loves you too much. Why don't you just open your door and let him in?"

...continued next page

5. LANGUAGE

Melissa tried this once. When Roger started yowling, she stomped across her room and opened the door. He bounded in. She lay back down, and tried to go to sleep. She couldn't. It isn't easy to sleep when a cat is walking on your head. She moved Roger, but he came back. She hid her head under her blanket, but he just poked her over and over again with his paw. When he started to yowl again, Melissa got fed up. She jerked the blanket off her head and stood up.

"Oh no you don't!" she said. "No yowling in here!" She put Roger out into the hall where he started his song again.

FREE RESPONSE

11. What does the underlined phrase mean? (3.L.4)

At night, Roger would sit outside her door <u>perched like a hen on an egg</u>.

_____

_____

_____

_____

_____

5.4. CHAPTER REVIEW

12. What does the underlined word mean? (3.L.4)

He <u>bounded</u> in.

_____

_____

_____

_____

_____

 prepaze

13. What does the underlined word mean? (3.L.4)

Every night, at around one in the morning, Roger would start to <u>yowl</u>.

_____

_____

_____

_____

_____

=== **TRUE OR FALSE** ===

14. Melissa's stomach literally twists up while she is trying to sleep. (3.L.4)

    A. True   **B.** False

15. When Roger started yowling, Melissa loudly and angrily walked across her room and opened the door. (3.L.4)

    A. True   **B.** False

> **Directions:** *Read the passage and answer the questions that follow.*

PROBLEM WITH PONIES

    Lights rise on Stacey and Jane, each eight years old, sitting cross-legged on the floor of Jane's playroom. The room is covered in pictures of ponies, toy ponies, and pony stuffed animals.

    Jane, whose clothes are also covered in ponies, forces a toy pony into Stacey's hand.

STACY
I don't like ponies!

...continued next page

    www.prepaze.com

5. LANGUAGE

JANE
Too bad. It's my house.
STACEY
But it's all we ever do.
JANE
I know! Isn't it great?
STACEY
No! I get tired of it.

=== **FREE RESPONSE** ===

16. **What do the names written in all capital letters represent?** (3.L.5)

_____

_____

_____

17. **How should the stage be decorated? How do you know?** (3.L.5)

_____

_____

_____

_____

_____

_____

_____

5. 4. CHAPTER REVIEW

prepaze

5. LANGUAGE

18. Where does this portion of the play take place? (3.L5)

_____

_____

_____

_____

_____

_____

_____

OUT WEST

Eliza stared out of the back of the covered wagon. Fields of grass stretched for miles and miles behind them. Eliza thought she had felt every single bump of the wagon along the way.

Riding in the back of the wagon was definitely not comfortable. She and her sister Martha were squeezed in among all of the family's belongings. Wooden chests held clothes and blankets. Crates held her mother's iron pots and pans. A barrel held bread and dried meat for the long journey.

Eliza sighed. She had been happy at their home in Ohio. But her father was eager to settle out west. There was rich farmland for the taking out there. He dreamed of a cabin and fields of corn. But Eliza missed her little house in Ohio. She missed her friends. She knew life on a farm was hard work. Would there even be a school out there?

Her father didn't seem to care about these things. "The Civil War is over," he said. "It's time for a fresh start for all of us." So they had packed up their belongings and joined the next wagon train out west.

...continued next page

5. LANGUAGE

Eliza was relieved when the wagon came to a stop. The wagons in the train formed a circle. It was time to get out, stretch, and cook the evening meal. The men had killed some wild pheasants the day before, so dinner would be tasty, at least.

Eliza hopped out of the wagon. They were in the middle of a prairie. Colorful flowers grew among the tall grasses. They made Eliza smile. She still wasn't happy about the move out west. But at least the flowers were pretty.

MULTIPLE CHOICE

19. **Who said, "Colorful flowers grew among the tall grasses."?** (3.L5)

    A. Eliza
    C. Martha
    B. Eliza's father
    D. The Narrator

TRUE OR FALSE

20. **The passage is written in the first person from Eliza's perspective.** (3.L5)

    A. True
    B. False

THE GOOSE THAT LAID THE GOLDEN EGGS

There once was a man who owned a wonderful goose. Every morning, the goose laid for him a big, beautiful egg — an egg made of pure, shiny, solid gold. Every morning, the man collected golden eggs. And little by little, egg by egg, he began to grow rich. But the man wanted more.

"My goose has all those golden eggs inside her," he kept thinking. "Why not get them all at once?"

One day he couldn't wait any longer. He grabbed the goose and killed her. But there were no eggs inside her!

"Why did I do that?" the man cried! "Now there will be no more golden eggs."

 prepaze

=== **FREE RESPONSE** ===

21. **Who is telling this story? How do you know?** (L.3.6)

_____

_____

_____

_____

_____

_____

22. **If you had a rooster that laid golden eggs how would your feelings be the same or different than the man?**

_____

_____

_____

_____

_____

_____

_____

5. LANGUAGE

23. **What does the narrator think of the man?** (L.3.6)

_____

_____

_____

_____

_____

_____

24. **What does the man think about the goose?** (L.3.6)

_____

_____

_____

_____

_____

_____

5. 4. CHAPTER REVIEW

prepaze

5. LANGUAGE

=== **TRUE OR FALSE** ===

25. The passage is written in the first person. (L.3.6)

    A. True   **B.** False

=== **FILL IN THE ANSWER** ===

26. The place where a novel takes place is called the _____. (L.3.6)

27. The special form that a play is written in is called a _____. (L.3.6)

28. An act is made up of smaller sections called _____. (L.3.6)

> ➤ *Directions: Read the passage and answer the questions.*

AMRA AND THE SKATEBOARD

The skateboard flew down the hill. Buzzing over the pavement, it passed by houses with manicured gardens and freshly cut grass, and whizzed past prim and proper homeowners—middle-aged mothers with beehive haircuts and stern-looking fathers with Oxford button-downs tucked into crisp khaki pants. At the bottom of the hill, it slammed into the curb and landed violently on its side.

Amra was searching for worms in her front yard. She was on her hands and knees when she heard the whizzing crack. Startled, she shot her head up and scanned the scene.

She saw the skateboard to her right, lying on the sidewalk. To her left, high up on the hill, she saw a gaggle of boys. Blinding rays of light carved out their silhouetted figures. The outlines of kneepads and helmets could be made out, as well as other skateboards, some held like canes, others like briefcases. One among the crew was sitting on his bottom, rocking back and forth in mild pain. He had wiped out.

Amra walked over to the skateboard. She took it into her hands and looked up toward the boys. One of them beckoned to her with his hand.

...continued next page

5. LANGUAGE

"Bring it up!" he called out.

The thought of interacting with them set her nerves on edge. She was only 10. They were older—high-schoolers.

Amra slowly walked the skateboard to the top. The boys stood there expressionless.

"Thanks kid," the one who wiped out said.

He walked over and took the skateboard from Amra's arms.

"Can I try?" she asked him.

The boys laughed.

"You're just a kid," Wipe Out said.

"And you're a girl," added another.

More laughter.

Amra shot an angry look. "Let me try!"

Wipe Out smirked. "Okay," he said, and handed back the skateboard.

Amra laid it on the pavement and rolled it back and forth to get the feel of the concrete. Stepping her left foot onto the front of the skateboard, she crouched and shot off, zipping down the hill and landing on a strip of grass along the sidewalk.

When she lifted the skateboard over her head in triumph, the boys were dumbfounded.

=== FREE RESPONSE ===

29. **Describe what the boy is doing in the following sentence.** (L.3.4)

One of them <u>beckoned</u> to her with his hand.

_____

_____

_____

_____

_____

30. Describe what the underlined phrase means in the following sentence. (L.3.4)

She saw a <u>gaggle</u> of boys.

_____

_____

_____

_____

_____

END OF YEAR ASSESSMENT

END OF YEAR ASSESSMENT

> **Directions:** *Read the passage and answer the questions below.*

EMPEROR'S NEW CLOTHES

Many years ago, there was an Emperor, who was so excessively fond of new clothes, that he spent all his money on them. He would not go anywhere unless he had the opportunity to display his new clothes. He had a different suit for each hour of the day. It if were any other king or emperor, people would say, "he is sitting on the throne." It was always said of him, "The Emperor is sitting in his wardrobe."

Time passed merrily in the large town and strangers arrived every day at the court. One day, two tricksters, calling themselves weavers, made their appearance. They said that they knew how to weave things of the most beautiful colors and patterns. The clothes they made have the wonderful power of remaining invisible to everyone who was unfit for their place in the king's office.

"These must, indeed, be splendid clothes!" thought the Emperor. "Had I such a suit, I might be able to see which men are unfit for their office, and also be able to know the wise from the foolish! This must be woven for me immediately." And he paid the weavers lots of money so they could begin their work.

So the two fake weavers set up two looms and pretended to work very busily, though they did nothing at all. They asked for the most delicate silk and the purest gold thread. They put both into their own knapsacks, and then continued their pretend work at the empty looms until late night.

END OF YEAR ASSESSMENT

MULTIPLE CHOICE

1. How does the text describe the Emperor? (RL.3.3)

A. humble and kind   **B.** proud and greedy
C. tall and slender   **D.** poor and needy

2. Why didn't the weavers make clothes for the Emperor? (RL.3.3)

A. They were not paid enough money.
B. They did not have enough silk or gold thread.
C. They did not have a loom to work with.
D. They were not real weavers.

TRUE OR FALSE

3. When writing a narrative, you should describe the thoughts and feelings of the characters. (W.3.3)

A. True   **B.** False

WRITING PROMPT

4. Write a narrative about a character who is afraid of a mysterious noise. Make sure to introduce and develop the characters, and provide a sense of closure. (W.3.3)

_____

_____

_____

_____

_____

_____

 prepaze

END OF YEAR ASSESSMENT

_____

_____

_____

_____

_____

_____

_____

_____

_____

_____

_____

_____

_____

_____

_____

_____

_____

END OF YEAR ASSESSMENT

> **Directions:** *Read the text and look at the picture. Answer the questions below.*

THE FIRST COLONY

A colony is an area that located in one country, but it is controlled by somewhere different. Jamestown Colony was the first colony in North America. A man named King James gave a group of wealthy men permission to start the colony. These 105 settlers came to Virginia in April 1607. They were there hoping to find gold. The place was called Jamestown in honor of King James. They faced many hardships during their time there, including fighting Native Americans, searching for food, and battling diseases. James Smith, James Rolfe, and Pocahontas were important to the colony's survival.

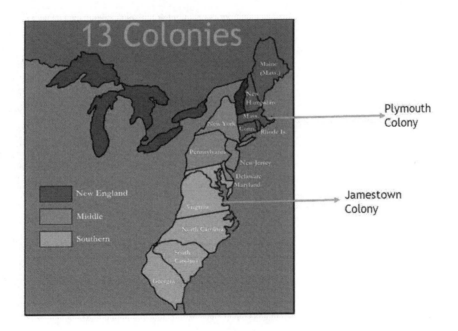

========== **MULTIPLE CHOICE** ==========

5. **Look at the map and map key. What type of colony was Jamestown?** (RI.3.7)

   A. New England   **B.** Middle   **C.** Southern   **D.** Plymouth

 prepaze

END OF YEAR ASSESSMENT

6. **Which of the following was NOT a problem faced by the Englishmen at Jamestown?** (RI.3.7)
    A. Battling disease
    B. Battling the Native Americans
    C. Finding food
    D. Looking for a buried treasure

7. **If you wanted to research the Plymouth Colony, which computer program would you use?** (W.3.6)
    A. Microsoft Word
    B. Email
    C. Internet
    D. Microsoft PowerPoint

> **Directions:** *Read the passage and answer the questions below.*

MICHAEL JORDAN

Michael Jordan's basketball career began well before he joined the NBA, but fans know him best for his success there. He played fifteen seasons in the National Basketball Association (NBA). During this time, he played for the Chicago Bulls and the Washington Wizards. There are many people who would argue that he is the best basketball player of all time.

Jordan played college basketball at the University of North Carolina. In 1984, he joined the Chicago Bulls. It did not take him long to rise to star status. "Air Jordan" and "His Airness" were just two of his many nicknames. Playing defense was one of his well-known talents.

In 1991, Jordan won his first NBA championship with the Chicago Bulls. His team repeated that victory in 1992 and 1993. In 1993, Jordan briefly retired from basketball. He decided to try out a new sport. His time as a baseball player did not last long. He returned to basketball in 1993 where he went back to the Chicago Bulls. He and his team earned three more championships in 1996, 1997, and 1998. In 1999, Jordan retired again. Once again, he just could not stay from the game. In 2002, he returned to the NBA to play for the Washington Wizards. He officially retired from the sport in 2003, leaving behind a legacy.

END OF YEAR ASSESSMENT

═══ **FILL IN THE BLANK** ═══

8. **Michael Jordan's basketball career began as a player for the**

    _____ . (RL.3.1)

9. **Michael Jordan quit playing basketball a total of _____ times throughout his career.** (RL.3.1)

═══ **WRITING PROMPT** ═══

10. **Imagine that you want to be a professional basketball player. Write a letter to Michael Jordan, explaining why he is an inspiration to you.** (W.3.4)

    _____

    _____

    _____

    _____

    _____

    _____

    _____

    _____

    _____

prepaze

END OF YEAR ASSESSMENT

> ➤ **Directions:** *Read the passage and answer the questions below.*

CALL IT COURAGE

"Mafatu is afraid of the sea. He will never be a warrior." Kana laughed again, and the scorn of his voice was like a spear thrust through Mafatu's heart. "Aia!" Kana was saying. "I have tried to be friendly with him. But he is good only for making spears. Mafatu is a coward."

The boys disappeared down the moonlit beach. Their laughter floated back on the night air. Mafatu stood quite still. Kana had spoken; he had voiced, once for all, the feeling of the tribe. Mafatu Stout Heart-was a coward. He was the Boy Who Was Afraid.

His hands were damp and cold. His nails dug into his palms. Suddenly a fierce resentment stormed through him. He knew in that instant what he must do: he must prove his courage to himself, and to the others, or he could no longer live in their midst. He must face Moana, the Sea God— face him and conquer him. He must.

The boy stood there taut as a drawn arrow awaiting its release. Off to the south somewhere there were other islands ... He drew a deep breath. If he could win his way to a distant island, he could make a place for himself among strangers. And he would never return to Hikueru until he should have proven himself! He would come back with his head high-held in pride, and he would hear his father say: "Here is my son Stout Heart. A brave name for a brave boy. "Standing there with clenched fists, Mafatu knew a smarting on his eyelids and shut his eyes tight, and sank his teeth into his lower lip.

═══════════ **MULTIPLE CHOICE** ═══════════

11. **Which words best describe the story's mood?** (RL.3.7)

     A. Lighthearted and playful   **B.** Dark and somber

     C. Silly and comical   **D.** Spooky and terrifying

12. **Which sentence(s) best demonstrate the story's mood?** (RL.3.7)

     A. The boys disappeared down the moonlit beach.

     B. Their laughter floated back on the night air.

     C. Mafatu stood quite still.

     D. All of the above

END OF YEAR ASSESSMENT

> **Directions:** *Read the passage and answer the questions below.*

THE NORTH WIND AND THE SUN

The North Wind and the Sun had an argument about which of them was stronger. While they were disputing with much heat and bluster, a traveler passed along the road wrapped in a cloak.

"Let us agree," said the Sun, "that whoever can strip that traveler of his cloak is the strongest."

"Very well," growled the North Wind. He sent a cold, howling blast against the traveler.

With the first gust of wind the ends of the cloak whipped about the traveler's body. But he immediately wrapped it closely around him, and the harder the Wind blew, the tighter he held it to himself. The North Wind tore angrily at the cloak, but all of his efforts were in vain.

Then the Sun began to shine. At first his beams were gentle. In the pleasant warmth after the bitter cold of the North Wind, the traveler unfastened his cloak and let it hang loosely from his shoulders. The Sun's rays grew warmer and warmer. The man took off his cap and mopped his brow. At last he became so heated that he pulled off his cloak, and, to escape the blazing sunshine, threw himself down in the welcome shade of a tree by the roadside.

Gentleness and kind persuasion win where force and aggression fail.

 prepaze

END OF YEAR ASSESSMENT

=== **FREE RESPONSE** ===

13. **Summarize the central message of the story.** (RL.3.2)

_____

_____

_____

_____

_____

_____

_____

_____

_____

_____

_____

_____

_____

END OF YEAR ASSESSMENT

END OF YEAR ASSESSMENT

14. How is the central message conveyed in the story (characters, plot, etc.)? (RL.3.2)

_____

_____

_____

_____

_____

_____

_____

_____

> **Directions:** _Look at the webpage and answer the questions below._

SPIDERS

Spiders are quite literally all around us. A recent entomological survey of North Carolina homes turned up spiders in 100 percent of them, including 68 percent of bathrooms and more than three-quarters of bedrooms. There's a good chance at least one spider is staring at you right now, sizing you up from a darkened corner of the room, eight eyes glistening in the shadows.

Spiders mostly eat insects, although some of the larger species have been known to snack on lizards, birds and even small mammals. Given their abundance and the voraciousness of their appetites, two European biologists recently wondered: If you were to tally up all the food eaten by the world's entire spider population in a single year, how much would it be?

Martin Nyffeler and Klaus Birkhofer published their estimate in the journal the Science of Nature earlier this month, and the number they arrived at is frankly shocking: The world's spiders consume somewhere between 400 _million_ and 800 million tons of prey in any given year. That means that spiders eat at least as much meat as all 7 billion humans on the planet combined, who the authors note consume about 400 million tons of meat and fish each year.

 prepaze

END OF YEAR ASSESSMENT

MULTIPLE CHOICE

15. **Where would you click to find more information about how many insects you may currently have in your room?** (RI.3.5)

A. 1   **B.** 2   **C.** 3   **D.** None of the above

16. **Where would you click to find more information about how much spiders eat in one year?** (RI.3.5)

A. 2   **B.** 3   **C.** 1   **D.** None of the above

WRITING PROMPT

17. **Write an informational text about spiders. Make sure to introduce, develop, and conclude your topic.** (W.3.2)

_____

_____

_____

_____

_____

_____

_____

_____

_____

prepaze   **www.prepaze.com**

END OF YEAR ASSESSMENT

> **Directions:** *Read the passage and answer the questions below.*

BACTERIA

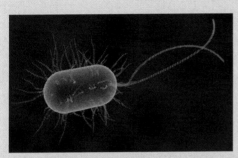

While some bacteria does make us sick, others are important for our health. Good bacteria help living beings thrive. They break down dead plants and animals, which then become nutrients for the soil. Without these nutrients, the soil would not be able to produce food for animals and humans.

Some foods are also unique because of the bacteria that live inside them. Some types of bread would have a different flavor and texture without bacteria. The same is true for yogurt and cheese.

Humans need bacteria too. Without the small bacteria that live in our stomachs and intestines, we would be unable to digest food. Bacteria are also responsible for removing dead skin cells which allow our pores to breathe. Scientists even rely on bacteria when making some medicines that help us recover from illnesses.

Undoubtedly, bacteria just might be the most beneficial living things on Earth! Without it, everything around us would be strangely different.

=== **MULTIPLE CHOICE** ===

18. **What does the word *thrive* most likely mean in this sentence?** (RI.3.4)

    Good bacteria help living beings <u>thrive</u>.

    A. Live and grow
    B. Perish and diet
    C. Become ill
    D. Gain energy

19. **What does the word beneficial most likely mean in this sentence?** (RI.3.4)

    Undoubtedly, bacteria just might be the most <u>beneficial</u> living things on Earth!

    A. Dreadful
    B. Tiny
    C. Popular
    D. Helpful

prepaze

END OF YEAR ASSESSMENT

> ➤ **Directions:** *Read the passages and answer the questions below.*

PASSAGE 1

What's your favorite food? A hearty soup? Spicy tacos? An earthy green salad? Have you ever considered where that food comes from? Let's take pizza for example. The soup comes from different ingredients that are grown on farms around the world. The spices used to add flavor to the soup come from herb gardens. Yes, that's right – a lot of your soup came straight from a plant. When you ate that bowl of hearty soup, you participated in a complex process of passing energy from plants to animals. This process is the called the food chain.

PASSAGE 2

The food chain begins with the sun. Without sunlight, plants cannot create their own food. This combined with water and carbon dioxide leads to a process known as photosynthesis. While the plant will use most of the energy that it makes, about ten percent of the energy will be stored for later use. This stored plant energy is passed on to humans and animals when we eat these plants. As a result, plants are the primary producers in a food chain.

=== **FILL IN THE BLANK** ===

20. **Both passages explain how plants and humans are part of the**

_____. (RI.3.9)

21. **Passage 2, offers more details about the _____'s role in the food chain than passage 2.** (RI.3.9)

END OF YEAR ASSESSMENT

> ➤ **Directions:** *Read the passage and answer the questions below.*

MY FATHER'S DRAGON

My father could see that the trail went through the clearing, so he decided to crawl around the edge in the underbrush and not disturb the lion.

He crawled and crawled, and the yelling grew louder and louder. Just as he was about to reach the trail on the other side the yelling suddenly stopped. My father looked around and saw the lion glaring at him. The lion charged and skidded to a stop a few inches away.

"Who are you?" the lion yelled at my father.

"My name is Elmer Elevator."

"Where do you think you're going?"

"I'm going home," said my father.

"That's what you think!" said the lion. "Ordinarily I'd save you for afternoon tea, but I happen to be upset enough and hungry enough to eat you right now." And he picked up my father in his front paws to feel how fat he was.

My father said, "Oh, please, Lion, before you eat me, tell me why you are so particularly upset today."

"It's my mane," said the lion, as he was figuring how many bites a little boy would make. "You see what a dreadful mess it is, and I don't seem to be able to do anything about it. My mother is coming over on the dragon this afternoon, and if she sees me this way I'm afraid she'll stop my allowance. She can't stand messy manes! But I'm going to eat you now, so it won't make any difference to you."

"Oh, wait a minute," said my father, "and I'll give you just the things you need to make your mane all tidy and beautiful. I have them here in my pack."

"You do?" said the lion. "Well, give them to me, and perhaps I'll save you for afternoon tea after all," and he put my father down on the ground.

END OF YEAR ASSESSMENT

=== **MULTIPLE CHOICE** ===

22. **Who is the narrator of this story?** (RL.3.6)
    A. The father in the story
    B. The child of the father in the story
    C. The lion
    D. The lion's mother

23. **From what point of view does the narrator tell the story?** (RL.3.6)
    A. First person
    B. Second person
    C. Third person limited
    D. Third person omniscient

=== **WRITING PROMPT** ===

24. **Write an opinion piece about the story My Father's Dragon. Make sure to state your opinion, list your reasons, and conclude your writing.** (RL.3.6,W.3.1)

_____

_____

_____

_____

_____

_____

_____

END OF YEAR ASSESSMENT

_____

_____

_____

_____

_____

_____

_____

_____

_____

> **Directions:** _Read the following article and answer the questions below._

ALLOW KIDS LESS TIME ON DIGITAL DEVICES

Most parents want their children to spend less time watching television. This is what the toy company, Melissa and Doug say. The company asked parents questions in a survey.

The parents also do not want kids playing on a phone or computer for long. They are right. Studies show that screen time can be bad for health. Using computers or phones can make people weigh too much. It also can be hard on a person's mind.

Parents need to stick to their limits. Parents can change some rules ahead of time. They might let kids use phones on long car rides. Still, if they have a rule against phones on school nights, they should follow it. If they change it once, kids might expect more. Kids might ask for screens the next night.

prepaze

END OF YEAR ASSESSMENT

=== **MULTIPLE CHOICE** ===

25. What is the issue being discussed in this article? (RI.3.6)

   A. The high cost of digital devices

   B. The increasing popularity of digital devices

   C. Banning digital devices for children

   D. Limiting the use of digital devices for children

26. What is the author's position on this issue? (RI.3.6)

   A. Parents should stop buying digital devices for their children.

   B. Parents should set rules when allowing their children to use digital devices.

   C. Parents should not let their children watch television.

   D. Parents should buy cell phones for their children.

=== **WRITING PROMPT** ===

27. Write a paragraph expressing your own opinion about the article. (W.3.1)

_____

_____

_____

_____

_____

_____

_____

END OF YEAR ASSESSMENT

> **Directions:** *Read the passage and answer the questions below.*

PETER PAN

Certainly Wendy had been dreaming.

But Wendy had not been dreaming, as the very next night showed, the night on which the extraordinary adventures of these children may be said to have begun.

On the night we speak of all the children were once more in bed. It happened to be Nana's evening off, and Mrs. Darling had bathed them and sung to them till one by one they had let go her hand and slid away into the land of sleep.

All were looking so safe and cozy that she smiled at her fears now and sat down by the fire to sew.

It was something for Michael, who on his birthday was getting new shirts. The fire was warm, however, and the nursery was dimly lit by three night-lights. Presently, the sewing lay on Mrs. Darling's lap. Then her head nodded, oh, so gracefully. She was asleep. Look at the four of them, Wendy and Michael over there, John here, and Mrs. Darling by the fire. There should have been a fourth night-light.

===== **MULTIPLE CHOICE** =====

28. **Fill in the blank:** (RL.3.4)

But Wendy had not been dreaming, as the very next night showed, the night on which the **extraordinary** adventures of these children may be said to have begun.

The word **extraordinary** most likely means_____

29. **Fill in the blank:** (RL.3.4)

Then her head nodded, oh, so **gracefully**. She was asleep.

The word **gracefully** most likely means_____

 prepaze

END OF YEAR ASSESSMENT

> ➤ **Directions:** *Read the passage and answer the questions below.*

HEART HEALTH

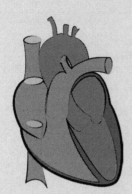

The human heart is one of the most important organs in the body. The main job of the heart is to pump blood to every part of the body. The blood carries oxygen, food, vitamins, and minerals that the body needs. The blood also removes the waste products that the body does not need. Each day, the average heart beats 100,000 times. It pumps out 2,000 gallons of blood. The heart is roughly the size of a fist. The heart does the most physical work than any muscle in the body. Because the heart helps our bodies work, we must keep our hearts healthy. Doctors recommend that we get plenty of exercises. They suggest that we get our heart rate up by exercising for at least 30 minutes each day. We can do these many different ways. We can walk, run, bike, lift weights, or play sports. We can also exercise while having fun playing with our friends. Think of all the times you are playing a game while running around the yard or playground. It is also important to spend less time sitting. People tend to spend hours sitting at their desks at work or school. People also sit for long periods of time while riding in cars. More time should be spent getting up out of our chairs and moving.

FREE RESPONSE

30. **According to the text, why is the heart one of the most important organs in the body?** (RI.3.1)

_____

_____

_____

_____

_____

END OF YEAR ASSESSMENT

> **Directions:** *Read the passages and answer the questions below.*

STORY 1

THE ELDERBUSH

"It is lovely here in autumn!" said the little girl. And suddenly the atmosphere grew as blue again as before. The forest grew red, and green, and yellow. The dogs came leaping along, and whole flocks of wild fowl flew over the hills. Blackberry bushes were hanging around the old stones. The sea was dark blue, covered with ships full of white sails. In the barn old women and children were sitting around. The young sang songs, but the old told fairy tales about magical creatures . Nothing could be more charming.

"It is delightful here in winter!" said the little girl. All the trees were covered with frost and they looked like white corals. The snow crackled under ones foot, as if they had new boots on. One falling star after the other was seen in the sky.

...continued next page

  prepaze

END OF YEAR ASSESSMENT

STORY 2

THE FIR TREE

"It is now winter outdoors!" thought the Tree. "The earth is hard and covered with snow. Men cannot plant me now, and therefore I have been put up here under shelter until the springtime comes! How thoughtful that is! How kind man is, after all! If it only were not so dark here, and so terribly lonely! Not even a hare! And out in the woods it was so pleasant when the snow was on the ground. The hare leaped by! Yes, even when he jumped over me, I did not like it then! It is really terribly lonely here!"

"Squeak! Squeak!" said a little Mouse, at the same moment, peeping out of his hole. And then another little one came. They sniffed about the Fir Tree, and rustled among the branches.

"It is dreadfully cold," said the Mouse. "But for that, it would be delightful here, old Fir,

wouldn't it?"

END OF YEAR ASSESSMENT

===== **TRUE OR FALSE** =====

31. Both stories create imagery about the weather. (RL.3.9)

    A. True   **B.** False

32. These stories feature the same characters in a different setting. (RL.3.9)

    A. True   **B.** False

> **Directions:** *Read the passage and answer the questions below.*

BATTERIES

We use batteries every day. They are important for helping us in our daily lives. They power our television remote controls, gaming systems, and iPods. Batteries are the power sources that supply energy to make devices turn on and off. Batteries provide us portable sources of energy. That means we can power our devices without wires or cables. We are free to move around with them. Without batteries, many of the devices we use while on the go would not work. By using batteries, we can watch videos on our phones while traveling.

===== **MULTIPLE CHOICE** =====

33. What is the main idea of this text? (RI.3.2)

    A. Batteries are important because they power portable devices.

    B. Batteries are not necessary for home device usage.

    C. Batteries are not important if you only use wires and cables.

    D. Most iPods require batteries.

34. Which of these sentences best demonstrate cause and effect? (RI.3.8)

    A. We use batteries every day.

    B. They power our television remote controls, gaming systems, and iPods.

    C. Without batteries, many of the devices we use while on the go would not work.

    D. Batteries provide us with portable sources of energy.

Copyrighted Material prepaze

END OF YEAR ASSESSMENT

> **Directions:** *Look at the play and answer the questions below.*

MACBETH

ACT I

SCENE I

Thunder and lightning.

ENTER THREE WITCHES

FIRST WITCH:	When shall we three meet again In thunder, lightning, or in rain?
SECOND WITCH:	When the hurlyburly's done, When the battle's lost and won
THIRD WITCH:	That will be at the set of sun.
FIRST WITCH:	Where is the place?
SECOND WITCH:	Upon the heath.
THIRD WITCH:	There to meet with Macbeth.
FIRST WITCH:	I come, Graymalkin!
SECOND WITCH:	Paddock calls.
THIRD WITCH:	Soon
ALL WITCHES:	Fair is foul, and foul is fair: Hover through the fog and filthy air.

EXIT WITCHES

SCENE II

Duncan's Castle

ENTER DUNCAN, CAPTAIN, MALCOLM, DONALBAIN, and LENNOX. CAPTAIN is bleeding and weak.

DUNCAN: What bloody man is that? He can report,
It seems by his troubles, of the revolt of the newest state.

MALCOM: This is the sergeant. Who like a good and hardy soldier
fought, Against my captivity. Hail, brave friend!
Say to the king your knowledge of the broil
As you did leave it.

DUNCAN: Doubtful it stood; As two drowning swimmers, that cling
together, And choke in the water.

prepaze   Copyrighted Material   **www.prepaze.com**

END OF YEAR ASSESSMENT

=== **FILL IN THE BLANK** ===

35. **The play is divided into parts called** _____. (RL.3.5)

36. **The scenes are part of a(n)** _____. (RL.3.5)

=== **FREE RESPONSE** ===

37. **Name at least five characters in this play.** (W.3.3.C)

_____

_____

_____

_____

_____

_____

_____

_____

_____

_____

Copyrighted Material **prepaze**

END OF YEAR ASSESSMENT

> **Directions:** *Read the text and answer the questions below.*

MOVIE THEATER HISTORY

When movie theaters first opened, the ticket price was only a nickel. These theaters were called nickelodeons. They got their name from the Greek word for theater and "nickel," referring to the ticket price. On June 19, 1905, the world's first nickelodeon theater opened in Pittsburgh, Pennsylvania. The theater had 96 seats and admission was just five cents. By 1907, about two million Americans had visited a nickelodeon.

Many of the films played in these early theaters were in black and white. They were silent and played only for a few minutes. They were nothing like the movies we enjoy today in large cinemas. Nickelodeons were soon replaced by larger theaters. When technology improved, these new theaters could play much longer films. In fact, they showed full-length feature films. This allowed them to charge higher admission prices from the five-cent ticket cost of the nickelodeons.

Larger theaters were now called movie palaces. On April 12, 1914, the first movie palace opened in New York. It seated around 3,000 people. A movie palace was known for its large size and fancy interior. Movie palaces had orchestra pits where musicians would play music to match the actions of the characters on screen.

=== **MULTIPLE CHOICE** ===

38. Which of these events happened first? (RI.3.3)

A. Theaters began to charge higher admission prices.

B. Millions of Americans began to visit movie theaters.

C. Theaters began to show longer movies.

D. Theaters began to increase in size.

prepaze   **www.prepaze.com**

END OF YEAR ASSESSMENT

39. How did new technology affect movie theaters? (RI.3.3)

A. New technology allowed movie theaters to play longer films.

B. New technology allowed people to play their own movies, instead of going to a theater.

C. New technology allowed movie theaters to charge lower ticket prices.

D. New technology did not affect movie theaters at all.

> **Directions:** *Read the question and write your answer in the space provided.*

40. Read the sentences. Revise in order to get rid of the repeated words. (W.3.5)

Did you bring the note? Did you bring the pen? Did you bring the watch?

_____

_____

_____

_____

_____

41. Look at the writing prompt. Complete the outline to plan your response. (W.3.5)

The local radio station is looking for a student to announce the weather. Write a speech about why you would be a good person to do this.

I. I really to do this because _____

II. I am good at _____

III. I am also good at _____

IV. You should pick me because _____

END OF YEAR ASSESSMENT

═══ **MULTIPLE CHOICE** ═══

42. You are trying to find out what made Rosa Parks famous. What resource should you use to complete the research? (W.3.7)

A. Dictionary **B.** Thesaurus **C.** Encyclopedia **D.** Blog

> **Directions:** *Joshua has one week to complete an essay. Each day, he will complete part of the writing process in class. Read his teacher's instructions and answer the questions below.*

MRS. JOHNSON'S CLASS

AMERICAN HISTORY ESSAY

Assignment details: You will select an important moment in American history and write an essay about the topic. The weekly writing schedule is as follows:

Day 1: Research your topic

Day 2: Create an outline of your paper

Day 3: Write a rough draft of your report

Day 4: Revise your report

Day 5: Final edits/submit the final draft

═══ **MULTIPLE CHOICE** ═══

43. Which sentence best describes what Joshua should do on Day 4? (W.3.10)

A. Joshua should write his final draft.

B. Joshua should finish researching his topic.

C. Joshua should make revisions to his rough draft.

D. Joshua should make revisions to his final draft.

END OF YEAR ASSESSMENT

44. Which of the following would be the best idea for making revisions to an essay? (W.3.10)

    A. Joshua asks the teacher for feedback on his essay.

    B. Joshua asks two classmates to read his essay and share their opinions.

    C. Joshua proofreads his essay and makes corrections.

    D. All of the above

➤ **Directions:** *Recall or look up information about any country. Sort your information in the chart below.*

45.

Country:
Language(s) spoken:
Flag color(s):
Popular foods:
Types of music enjoyed:

 prepaze

ANSWER KEY

ANSWER KEY

1. READING: LITERATURE

1.1. Key Ideas and Details

1. Answer: C

Explanation: The sentence "They were rewarded by two discoveries" best describes what happened during the children's long walk. The children saw a hollow tree filled with walnuts and a runaway hen.

2. Answer: A

Explanation: The children first discovered a hollow tree.

3. Answer: D

Explanation: The second discovery was a runaway hen.

4. Answer: B

Explanation: The children were alarmed by the second discovery at first.

5. Answer: A

Explanation: The sentence "The other discovery frightened them a little just at first" best describes how the children felt about the second discovery.

6. Answer: A

Explanation: The sentence "Jess bent over incredulously and saw a rude nest in the moss in which there were five eggs" best describes where the children found the eggs.

7. Answer: Answers will vary

Explanation: The text states, "The children had no scruples at all about taking the eggs." Students should be able to recognize that the children felt positive about their decision to take the eggs based on text evidence.

8. Answer: A

Explanation: The Fox wanted to amuse himself by making fun of the Stork.

9. Answer: C

Explanation: The text states that Stork was displeased, or unhappy, with Fox's trick.

10. Answer: B

Explanation: The sentence "The hungry Stork was much displeased at the trick, but he was a calm, even-tempered fellow and saw no good in flying into a rage" best describes how Stork felt about Fox's trick.

11. Answer: B

Explanation: The Stork invited the Fox to dinner.

12. Answer: D

Explanation: The Stork wanted to play a trick on the Fox.

13. Answer: B

Explanation: The central message of a story is a lesson or moral that the author wants to convey. The central message of this story is: Do not play tricks on others if you do not like to be tricked.

14. Answer: A

Explanation: Timmy Willie is kind to Johnny Town-mouse, based on events described in the story.

15. Answer: C

Explanation: The word polite best describes the character Timmy Willie.

16. Answer: B

Explanation: The sentence, "Timmy Willie received him with open arms." shows that Timmy's character is kind and polite towards Johnny.

17. Answer: B

Explanation: According to the text, Timmy prefers to live in the country.

prepaze

ANSWER KEY

18. Answer: D

Explanation: The sentence, "He went back in the very next hamper of vegetables; he said it was too quiet" best shows that Johnny did not want to live in the country.

19. Answer: A

Explanation: This statement is true. Johnny most likely did not like the loud noises in the country.

20. Answer: B

Explanation: This statement is true. Johnny most likely did not like the loud noises in the country.

1.2. Craft and Structure

1. Answer: D

Explanation: The word environment means the things in nature's surroundings.

2. Answer: A

Explanation: The word reuse means to use again.

3. Answer: B

Explanation: The word reduction is the act of making something smaller (less).

4. Answer: C

Explanation: The phrase let's take a minute literally means to allow time for something.

5. Answer: B

Explanation: The phrase one man's trash is another man's treasure literally means that someone else may want something that you don't want.

6. Answer: A

Explanation: This statement is true. An idiom is a figure of speech that uses words to express something other than the literal meaning.

7. Answer: B

Explanation: This statement is false. Figurative language uses figures of speech to express ideas.

8. Answer: B

Explanation: The poem is divided into sections called stanzas.

9. Answer: B

Explanation: A stanza is a group of lines in a poem. This poem has 3 stanzas.

10. Answer: C

Explanation: Each stanza contains a set of lines in this poem.

11. Answer: D

Explanation: The line *When the air does laugh with our merry wit* appears in stanza 1.

12. Answer: A

Explanation: The line *To sing the sweet chorus of 'Ha ha he!'* appears in the final line of the poem.

13. Answer: Answers will vary

Explanation: Students should demonstrate an understanding of how poems are divided into stanzas and write a poem with 2 stanzas.

14. Answer: C

Explanation: In the third person point of view, the narrator tells a story about someone else. The narrator in this text speaks in the third person point of view.

15. Answer: D

Explanation: The sentence "Once upon a time there were three little pigs and the time came for them to leave home and seek their fortunes" best helps to identify the narrator's point of view. The narrator tells the story.

16. Answer: C

Explanation: The narrator knows the wolf's thoughts and feelings.

1. READING: LITERATURE

ANSWER KEY

17. Answer: B

Explanation: The phrase "This made the wolf angry" shows that the narrator knows the wolf's thought and feelings.

18. Answer: Answers will vary

Explanation: Students should demonstrate an understanding of the first person point of view in their writing.

19. Answer: B

Explanation: This statement is false. The wolf is not narrating the story.

20. Answer: A

Explanation: This statement is true. The story is told from the third person point of view.

1.3. Integration of Knowledge and Ideas

1. Answer: D

Explanation: The story's mood is best described as frightening.

2. Answer: C

Explanation: The sentence "Her first thought was one of fear; her second, hope for shelter." helps to identify the story's mood.

3. Answer: A

Explanation: The freight car is best described as rugged.

4. Answer: B

Explanation: The sentence "It stood on rusty broken rails which were nearly covered with dead leaves" best describes the freight car.

5. Answer: Answers will vary

Explanation: Students should demonstrate an understanding of the way authors use language to appeal to a reader's senses. In this story, the author uses sensory language such as darkness, rusty, and "thunder cracks."

6. Answer: A

Explanation: This statement is true. The story's mood can be described as eerie.

7. Answer: B

Explanation: This statement is false. The author does not create joyful imagery in the story.

8. Answer: A

Explanation: This statement is false. Jess's mood is best described as curious.

9. Answer: A

Explanation: This statement is true. The author uses descriptive language in the story.

10. Answer: A

Explanation: Peter Rabbit and Benjamin Bunny are characters in both stories.

11. Answer: B

Explanation: Mr. McGregor's garden is a setting in both stories.

12. Answer: C

Explanation: Mrs. McGregor does not appear in both stories.

13. Answer: D

Explanation: Both stories take place outdoors.

14. Answer: B

Explanation: Benjamin is older in Story 2.

ANSWER KEY

15. Answer: A
Explanation: These stories are written by the same author.

16. Answer: A
Explanation: This statement is true. Benjamin Bunny is a main character in both stories.

17. Answer: A
Explanation: This statement is true. There is a conflict (or problem) in both stories. In Story 1, Peter has lost his shoes and coat in Mr. McGregor's garden. In Story 2, Benjamin Bunny needed lettuce from Mr. McGregor's garden.

18. Answer: B
Explanation: TThis statement is false. The mouse character appears in both stories

19. Answer: B
Explanation: This statement is false. Both stories are written by the same author.

20. Answer: A
Explanation: This statement is true. Two stories with the same characters can have different plots.

1.4. Chapter Review

1. Answer: B
Explanation: The word *historic* means famous in the context of this text.

2. Answer: C
Explanation: The word *machinery* means equipment in the context of this text.

3. Answer: B
Explanation: The word monitored means watched in the context of this text.

4. Answer: D
Explanation: The word *habitable* means livable in the context of this text.

5. Answer: D
Explanation: The dragon could not go back to his cloud for all of these reasons.

6. Answer: B
Explanation: The animals wanted to use the dragon to cross the river.

7. Answer: C
Explanation: The cat thinks of the dragon as a friend, according to the text.

8. Answer: A
Explanation: He was as big as a black bear.

9. Answer: C
Explanation: The word persistent best describes the narrator's father.

10. Answer: C
Explanation: The sentence, "My father tugged and tugged, and nearly pulled his boots right off" best demonstrates this character as persistent.

11. Answer: B
Explanation: The narrator left the beach because the jungle was too thick.

12. Answer: A
Explanation: The poem's imagery is best described as natural.

13. Answer: D
Explanation: The author uses descriptive language to create imagery.

14. Answer: A
Explanation: This statement is true. The poem can be described as blissful and happy.

15. Answer: B
Explanation: This statement is false. The author does use an angry tone in his writing.

1. READING: LITERATURE

prepaze

ANSWER KEY

16. Answer: second
Explanation: This article is written in the second person point of view.

17. Answer: positive
Explanation: The writer most likely has a positive opinion about the topic.

18. Answer: Answers will vary
Explanation: Students should demonstrate the ability to distinguish their own point of view from that of the author.

19. Answer: C
Explanation: Anansi did not want to wait for beans.

20. Answer: A
Explanation: Anansi hid beans under his hat.

21. Answer: D
Explanation: Anansi was greedy and wanted the beans for himself.

22. Answer: C
Explanation: The central message of a story is a lesson or moral that the author wants to convey. The central message of this story is: There are consequences to dishonesty and greed.

23. Answer: A
Explanation: A verse is a group of lyrics in a song. There are 3 verses in this song.

24. Answer: C
Explanation: The flag is the common theme in each verse.

25. Answer: B
Explanation: This statement is false. The song is divided into parts called verses.

26. Answer: B
Explanation: Verses 1 and 3 are longer. They both have 12 lines. Verse 2 has 9 lines.

27. Answer: B
Explanation: Both stories have trees and other elements of nature.

28. Answer: C
Explanation: The seasons change in both stories.

29. Answer: D
Explanation: One takes place in the woods, the other takes place in a garden.

30. Answer: A
Explanation: The tree in Story 2 is personified (or acts like a human).

2. READING: INFORMATIONAL TEXT

2.1. Key Ideas and Details

1. Answer: B
Explanation: The text says that Harriet was born in Maryland. She was born a slave and had to escape to the North where slavery was illegal.

2. Answer: B
Explanation: The text says that Harriet worked on a large plantation in the fields.

3. Answer: C
Explanation: The text says that to escape slavery, Harriet knew she had to travel to the North.

4. Answer: A
Explanation: The text says that Harriet traveled by night so she would not be caught leaving the plantation.

5. Answer: D
Explanation: The text says that Harriet walked nearly 90 miles by foot.

prepaze   Copyrighted Material   **www.prepaze.com**

ANSWER KEY

6. Answer: B
Explanation: The text says that the Underground Railroad was not a railroad at all. It was a secret path slaves would follow to run away.

7. Answer: D
Explanation: The text says by using railway terms, the people helping the escaped slaves could safely lead them in the right direction.

8. Answer: A
Explanation: The main topic of this text is that taste buds help us taste our food.

9. Answer: B
Explanation: The text says taste buds let us know how something tastes by sending messages to our brains.

10. Answer: D
Explanation: The text says the sides of the tongue can detect these tastes the best.

11. Answer: B
Explanation: The text says our sense of taste combines with our sense of smell.

12. Answer: C
Explanation: The key details further explain how taste buds help us taste our food.

13. Answer: C
Explanation: The text says that in order to make a Hawaiian pizza, you must follow a series of steps.

14. Answer: C
Explanation: The text lists seven steps.

15. Answer: A
Explanation: The text says that the first step is to build your layers.

16. Answer: B
Explanation: The text says that the second step is to flatten the dough.

17. Answer: C
Explanation: The text says that the third step is to spread the tomato sauce.

18. Answer: D
Explanation: The text says that you should bake the pizza for 10 minutes.

19. Answer: C
Explanation: The text states that you should remove the pizza from the oven.

20. Answer: A
Explanation: Each step leads to the next step in order to create a Hawaiian pizza.

2.2. Craft and Structure

1. Answer: B
Explanation: The phrase *physical characteristics* most likely refer to body features in the context of this text.

2. Answer: C
Explanation: The word *violently* would best replace the word viciously in this sentence.

3. Answer: A
Explanation: The word *accurate* most likely means exactly in the context of this text.

4. Answer: D
Explanation: The word *spawning* most likely means breeding in the context of this text.

5. Answer: C
Explanation: The phrase "tiger of the sea" is most likely a comparison between tigers and barracudas based on hunting skills.

6. Answer: B
Explanation: The word navigate most likely means travel in the context of this text.

2. READING: INFORMATIONAL TEXT

ANSWER KEY

7. Answer: A

Explanation: This text could also be titled "Savage Barracudas." The words savage has a similar meaning to the word brutal.

8. Answer: C

Explanation: The title of this webpage is "Animals." A website consists of a collection of pages. This is a webpage about animals on the National Geographic Kids website.

9. Answer: D

Explanation: You could use all of these features in order to access information about mammals on this website.

10. Answer: A

Explanation: You would click on the area titled "Mammals: Orca" if wanted to access information about whales. An orca is a type of whale.

11. Answer: B

Explanation: The advertisement link contains information about the novel Riders of the Realm.

12. Answer: C

Explanation: The website menu contains a list of other topics available on the website.

13. Answer: D

Explanation: The "join" button most likely refers to some type of membership or subscription related to the website.

14. Answer: A

Explanation: The article explores the possible dangers of diets for children.

15. Answer: B

Explanation: The author's position is that Weight Watchers should not market its programs to children.

16. Answer: C

Explanation: The author uses the fact that diets can lead to eating disorders to support her argument.

17. Answer: D

Explanation: The author mentions the American Academy of Pediatrics and its report on the effects of dieting to support her argument.

18. Answer: C

Explanation: The statement, "Diets can help to prevent obesity and poor health" does not support the author's argument.

19. Answer: A

Explanation: The author most likely believes that children should focus on good health instead of weight loss.

20. Answer: Answers will vary

Explanation: Students should demonstrate the ability to distinguish their own point of view from that of the author of a text.

2.3. Integration of Knowledge and Ideas

1. Answer: In the 1500s

Explanation: The text states that in the 1500s, Spain sent ships to the Americas

2. Answer: The first settlement

Explanation: The text states that when they came back, the men created the first settlement.

3. Answer: The Atlantic Ocean

Explanation: According to the map, the settlement was close to the Atlantic Ocean.

4. Answer: They couldn't find food and shelter

Explanation: The text states that after struggling to find food and shelter, the sailors went back to England.

5. Answer: North Carolina

Explanation: According to the map, the Lost Roanoke settlement was located in North Carolina.

prepaze

ANSWER KEY

6. Answer: D
Explanation: According to the text, the men arrived at the Americas first.

7. Answer: C
Explanation: According to the text, the 114 men disappeared last.

8. Answer: A
Explanation: These sentences demonstrate cause and effect. The rain caused the cancellation of the game.

9. Answer: C
Explanation: These sentences demonstrate problem and solution. The sunglasses are used as a solution to the bright sun.

10. Answer: A
Explanation: These sentences demonstrate a sequence of events. First, we went to the movies, then we went to the zoo.

11. Answer: Answers will vary
Explanation: Students should be able to explain the logical connection between sentences. These sentences compare and contrast cars.

12. Answer: Answers will vary
Explanation: Students should be able to explain the logical connection between sentences. These sentences explain how one action led to another. A car hit a bump, which caused it to run off the track.

13. Answer: A
Explanation: This statement is true. Both passages present information about the Amazon Rainforest.

14. Answer: B
Explanation: This statement is false. Both passages do not present information about how plants from Amazon Rainforest are used to make medicine; only the first passage talks about medicine.

15. Answer: B
Explanation: This statement is false. Passage 1 does not offer more geographical information about the Amazon Rainforest than passage 2.

16. Answer: B
Explanation: This statement is false. Passage 2 focuses more on the production of oxygen in the Amazon Rainforest than passage 1.

17 Answer: A
Explanation: This statement is true. Both passages explain how the Amazon Rainforest is useful to humans.

18. Answer: B
Explanation: Passage 1 states that there are many types of plants found in the Amazon Rainforest.

19. Answer: D
Explanation: Passage 2 states that covering a lot of Brazil and parts of Colombia, Peru, and some other South American countries, this is the world's biggest tropical rainforest.

20. Answer: A
Explanation: Both passages state that the Amazon Rainforest is located in South America.

2.4. Chapter Review

1. Answer: B
Explanation: The word *spacecraft* most likely refers to a vehicle used to travel into outer space.

2. Answer: A
Explanation: The phrase *plate tectonics* most likely refers to the structure of the earth's layers, based on the definition from the text.

 prepaze

ANSWER KEY

2. READING: INFORMATIONAL TEXT

3. Answer: C

Explanation: The phrase *magnetic* field most likely refers to an area of magnetic force.

4. Answer: C

Explanation: The word *shorelines* most likely "natural lines that separate oceans and shores, or land"

5. Answer: B

Explanation: The text discusses the issue of food companies offering money to schools in exchange for junk food labels.

6. Answer: B

Explanation: The author's position is that labels-for-cash programs can raise money, but may promote unhealthy food habits.

7. Answer: B

Explanation: The author uses the fact that health experts say that label programs are just a way to sell junk food to kids.
Explanation: to support the argument.

8. Answer: Answers will vary

Explanation: Students should be able to distinguish their own point of view from that of the author of a text.

9. Answer: B

Explanation: This statement is false. The phrase reduce, reuse, and recycle is known as the three R's.

10. Answer: B

Explanation: This statement is false. According to the text, we should reduce, reuse, and recycle daily.

11. Answer: A

Explanation: This statement is true. The text states that if we reduce, reuse, and recycle, we will limit the amount of waste we make.

12. Answer: Answers will vary

Explanation: Students should be able to answer questions by referring to the text.

The text states that books can be reused by protecting them with a cover.

13. Answer: D

Explanation: It takes at least 8 hours to reach the larval stage.

14. Answer: A

Explanation: The diagram shows that the house fly enters the pupa stage after the larval stage.

15. Answer: A

Explanation: The least amount of time is spent as an egg.

16. Answer: Answers will vary

Explanation: Students should be able to identify the main topic of a text. This text is mainly about the importance and benefits of composting.

17. Answer: Answers will vary

Explanation: Students should be able to explain how details support the main idea of a text. In this text, supporting details help to explain why composting is important. The students need to list at least 3 details.

18. Answer: B

Explanation: The topic of this article is that the net weight of insects consumed yearly by the world's spiders is greater than the combined net weight of living humans.

19. Answer: D

Explanation: Chris Murphy is the author of this article.

20. Answer: C

Explanation: This article was published by The Sun.

21. Answer: Amazon Rainforest

Explanation: Both passages explain how resources from the Amazon Rainforest are used to make other things.

ANSWER KEY

22. Answer: 1
Explanation: Passage 1 explains how plants are used to make medicine.

23. Answer: 2
Explanation: Passage 2 explains how plants are used to make rubber.

24. Answer: A
Explanation: They are honored with monuments and currency.

25. Answer: C
Explanation: In 1775, Washington was elected Commander in Chief of the Continental Army.

26. Answer: Answers will vary
Explanation: Students should be able to explain the relationship between a series of historical events. Lincoln issued the Emancipation Proclamation which gave slaves freedom in some states.

27. Answer: D
Explanation: All of these sentences demonstrate problem and solution.

28. Answer: B
Explanation: These sentences demonstrate cause and effect. The wind caused the tree to fall.

29. Answer: Answers will vary
Explanation: Students should be able to show a logical connection between sentences in a paragraph. Students should list a sequence of events in their writing.

30. Answer: Answers will vary
Explanation: Students should be able to show a logical connection between sentences in a paragraph. Students should compare and contrast in their writing.

3. READING: FOUNDATIONAL SKILLS

3.1. Phonics and Word Recognition

1. Answer: C
Explanation: The suffix -er means "a person who." A teacher is a person who teaches.

2. Answer: B
Explanation: The suffix -ly means "in a certain way." The word *mildly* means "in a mild way."

3. Answer: B
Explanation: The suffix -less means "without" The word *hopeless* means "without hope."

4. Answer: A
Explanation: The prefix dis- means "not" or "opposite." The word *disobey* means the opposite of obey.

5. Answer: D
Explanation: The suffix -y means "having or made of."

6. Answer: surely
Explanation: The word *surely* has an irregular spelling. Irregularly spelled words have letters that make an unusual sound. In the word *surely*, the letter s makes the /sh/ sound.

7. Answer: talented
Explanation: The word *talented* has 3 syllables. A syllable is a single unit of sound that has one vowel sound. The word *talented* is divided into three syllables (ta + lent + ed).

8. Answer: spicy, crunchy
Explanation: The suffix -y means "having or made of." The words *spicy* and *crunchy*

prepaze

3. READING: FOUNDATIONAL SKILLS

ANSWER KEY

have the suffix -y added to the base words *spice* and *crunch*. They describe something as having spice and crunch.

9. Answer: A

Explanation: This statement is true. The word *exam* is an irregularly spelled word. The letter /x/ makes the /z/ sound in this word.

10. Answer: B

Explanation: This statement is false. The word almost has 2 syllables. (al + most)

11. Answer: B

Explanation: This statement is false. The Latin suffix -or means "a person or thing who."

12. Answer: A

Explanation: This statement is true. The double consonant *ss* makes the /sh/ sound in the word *mission*.

13. Answer: B

Explanation: This statement is false. There is 1 vowel sound in each syllable of a word.

14. Answer: A

Explanation: The word *watermelon* has 4 syllables (wa + ter + mel + on).

15. Answer: B

Explanation: The word *yesterday* should be divided as follows: yes + ter + day. Based on the vc/v rule, the word should be divided after the consonant that follows each short vowel sound.

16. Answer: C

Explanation: The letters *qu* make the /k/ sound the in the word *conquer*.

17. Answer: unsafe

Explanation: The prefix un- means "not. It is very unsafe to ride a bike without a helmet.

18. Answer: fearless

Explanation: The suffix -less means "without." She looked fearless as she bravely climbed the mountain.

19. Answer: quickly

Explanation: The suffix -ly means "in a certain way." She quickly ran away from the angry dog.

20. Answer: preheat

Explanation: The prefix pre- means "before." The first step is to preheat the oven.

3.2. Chapter Review

1. Answer: B

Explanation: The Latin suffix -or means "a person or thing who." Visitors are people who visit.

2. Answer: C

Explanation: The prefix dis- means "not" or "opposite." The word *disrespectful* means "not respectful."

3. Answer: D

Explanation: There are 4 syllables in the word *activity* (ac + tiv + i + ty).

4. Answer: A

Explanation: The word *climbing* has an irregular spelling. The letter b is silent and the letter i makes the long /i/ without a silent e.

5. Answer: C

Explanation: The vowel blend *or* makes the /er/ sound in the word *worship*.

6. Answer: A

Explanation: This statement is true. The word *leaders* means "people who lead."

7. Answer: B

Explanation: This statement is false. The word *officials* is an irregularly spelled word. The letter c makes the /sh/ sound in this word.

ANSWER KEY

8. Answer: B
Explanation: This statement is false. The word *community* has 4 syllables (com + mu + ni + ty).

9. Answer: regions
Explanation: The word *regions* has an irregular spelling. The letter g make the /j/ sound and the vowel blend *io* makes the short /u/ sound.

10. Answer: flexible
Explanation: The Latin suffix -ible means "can do or can be." The word *flexible* means "able to flex or move."

11. Answer: repeat
Explanation: The prefix re- means "again." The word repeat means "to say something again."

12. Answer: colorful
Explanation: The word *colorful* has 3 syllables (col + or + ful).

13. Answer: A
Explanation: A syllable is a single unit of sound in a word.

14. Answer: B
Explanation: There is one vowel sound in each syllable of a word.

15. Answer: C
Explanation: A prefix can be added to the beginning of a word to change its meaning.

16. Answer: B
Explanation: An irregularly spelled word has letters that make unusual sounds.

17. Answer: helpful
Explanation: The suffix -ful means "full of." A dictionary can be helpful when learning new words.

18. Answer: actor
Explanation: The Latin suffix -or means "a person on thing who." The actor took a bow at the end of the play.

19. Answer: disappear
Explanation: The prefix dis- changes a word to its opposite meaning. The clouds seem to disappear at night.

20. Answer: creamy
Explanation: The suffix -y means "having or made of." The pudding was smooth and creamy.

21. Answer: A
Explanation: The word *special* has an irregular spelling. The letter c makes the /sh/ sound in this word.

22. Answer: D
Explanation: The word dentist is a regularly spelled word with no unusual sounds.

23. Answer: C
Explanation: The word adorable has a Latin suffix. The suffix -able is a Latin suffix that means "can do or can do."

24. Answer: B
Explanation: The suffix -er means "a person who." A speaker is a person who speaks.

25. Answer: A
Explanation: The suffix -ly means "in a certain way." The word *silently* means in a silent way."

26. Answer: C
Explanation: The word alligator has 4 syllables (al + li + ga + tor).

27. Answer: D
Explanation: The word *rocketship* should be divided as follows: roc + ket + ship. Based on the vc/v rule, the word should be divided after the consonant that follows each short vowel sound.

28. Answer: D
Explanation: The word *motorboat* should be divided as follows: mo + tor + boat.

prepaze

ANSWER KEY

Based on the v/cv rule, the word should be divided before the consonant that follows each long vowel sound. Also, an r-controlled vowel and the letter r should stay in the same syllable.

29. Answer: C

Explanation: The consonant s makes the /z/ sound in the word business.

30. Answer: A

Explanation: The vowel blend *ea* and the letter r make the /ar/ sound in the word *hearty*.

4. WRITING

4.1. Text Types and Purposes

1. Answer: B

Explanation: This statement is false. Opinion pieces are not based on fact or knowledge about a topic or text.

2. Answer: A

Explanation: This statement is true. When you write an opinion piece, you give your point of view on a topic and support your opinion with a list of reasons.

3. Answer: B

Explanation: The word *therefore* is a linking word in this sentence.

4. Answer: A

Explanation: By stating "my point of view", the writer is telling the reader that they are giving their opinion about a topic.

5. Answer: C

Explanation: By writing that President Lincoln was a good man, the writer is giving their opinion. All the other statements are facts.

6. Answer: A

Explanation: The sentence "To summarize, summer is the best season for surfing" is the best concluding statement.

7. Answer: C

Explanation: The sentence "As you can see, I have listed many reasons why football is an unsafe sport" is not an introductory statement.

8. Answer: Answers will vary

Explanation: Students should demonstrate the ability to write about their opinion on a specific topic.

9. Answer: B

Explanation: The word *but* is a linking word in this sentence.

10. Answer: D

Explanation: The statement "rainbows are made from sunlight that passes through water" is a fact. All the other statements are opinions or are about stories.

11. Answer: D

Explanation: This is the only informative choice. All others imply an opinion or for the writer to tell a story.

12. Answer: A

Explanation: This statement is true. If you were writing about how to make candles, you would be writing an explanatory text.

13. Answer: A

Explanation: This statement is true. Informative texts are based on facts, definitions, and details.

14. Answer: B

Explanation: This statement is false. This sentence is an example of a concluding statement.

15. Answer: Answers will vary

Explanation: Students should demonstrate the ability to write an explanatory text about a specific topic.

ANSWER KEY

16. Answer: C

Explanation: The word *after* is a temporal word.

17. Answer: D

Explanation: This is the only sentence that tells a story about three characters going to the zoo.

18. Answer: A

Explanation: This sentence describes the character's feelings and actions.

19. Answer: A

Explanation: This statement is true. This is an example of a narrative conclusion.

20. Answer: Answers will vary

Explanation: Students should demonstrate the ability to write a narrative about a personal experience.

4.2. Production and Distribution of Writing

1. Answer: B

Explanation: This opening sentence would be an appropriate way to address the person at the museum.

2. Answer: A

Explanation: This opening sentence is the best way to describe a time when you were scared.

3. Answer: D

Explanation: This opening sentence would be the best way to start a letter to your grandma.

4. Answer: A

Explanation: This opening sentence is the best way to try to persuade the reader about milk choices.

5. Answer: Answers will vary

Explanation: Students should be able to produce writing that is appropriate to task and purpose.

6. Answer: Answers will vary

Explanation: Students should be able to produce writing that is appropriate to task and purpose.

7. Answer: Have you ever seen a fossil?

Explanation: The "H" in have must be capitalized since it is the beginning of the question. Also, a question mark is required at the end of this question/interrogative sentence.

8. Answer: Last year, my family and I were on vacation.

Explanation: The "L" in last must be capitalized since it is the beginning of the sentence. Also, when referring to other people and oneself (I, me, etc), the other people are always listed first.

9. Answer: I found a fossil inside a rock.

Explanation: "I" should be capitalized because it is the beginning of the sentence, and it is a proper pronoun; 'rock' is not a proper noun, since it does not refer to anything specific. It should not be capitalized.

10. Answer: It felt rough and different from the rest of the rock.

Explanation: This sentence is not asking a question, so it should end with a period. There is no question.

11. Answer: Answers will vary

Explanation: Students should be able to plan and organize ideas in the form of an outline before writing. For example, I would like to eat vegetables because eating vegetables provides health benefits . I like to eat spinach because spinach keeps your brain young and healthy.

4. WRITING

ANSWER KEY

12. Answer: Answers will vary

Explanation: Students should be able to plan and organize ideas in the form of an outline before writing. The book was called The Adventures of Tom Sawyer. My favorite character was Tom Sawyer.

13. Answer: The brown dog has a white nose and brown eyes.

Explanation: By combining the details into a single sentence, you get rid of the repetitious phrase 'the dog.'

14. Answer: My friends, Lily, Tessa, and Becky, will be here soon.

Explanation: Since all three friends 'will be here soon', it is best to change 'friend' to 'friends' and then list their names combined with the conjunction 'and' in a series and separated by commas.

15. Answer: B

Explanation: Microsoft PowerPoint is the best program for creating a presentation.

16. Answer: C

Explanation: The internet is the best program for conducting research.

17. Answer: D

Explanation: Sending a question to a teacher would best be sent via email.

18. Answer: A

Explanation: Microsoft Word is a word processing program that is best for typing a short story.

19. Answer: Answers will vary

Explanation: Students should be able to explain how to use technology, such as the internet, to conduct research.

20. Answer: Answers will vary

Explanation: Students should be able to explain how to use technology, such as word processing programs, to produce writing.

4.3. Research to Build and Present Knowledge

1. Answer: D

Explanation: The internet would be the best way to look up information about Harriet Tubman.

2. Answer: C

Explanation: A map would be the quickest way to look up information about states and their capital cities.

3. Answer: D

Explanation: The internet would be the quickest way to look up this information.

4. Answer: B

Explanation: A thesaurus is a book used to look up synonyms and antonyms.

5. Answer: George Washington

Explanation: The keywords needed for the search would be who or what the sentence is mostly about. This is the focus and all other words are unnecessary for the search.

6. Answer: Siberian Husky

Explanation: The keywords needed for the search would be who or what the sentence is mostly about. This is the focus and all other words are unnecessary for the search.

7. Answer: Ferrari

Explanation: The keywords needed for the search would be who or what the sentence is mostly about. This is the focus and all other words are unnecessary for the search.

8. Answer: Stalagmites, stalactites

Explanation: The keywords needed for the search would be who or what the sentence is mostly about. This is the focus and all other words are unnecessary for the search.

4. WRITING

prepaze

www.prepaze.com

ANSWER KEY

9. Answer: Cape Cod, Massachusetts
Explanation: The keywords needed for the search would be who or what the sentence is mostly about. This is the focus and all other words are unnecessary for the search.

10. Answer: Seashells, Sanibel Island
Explanation: The keywords needed for the search would be who or what the sentence is mostly about. This is the focus and all other words are unnecessary for the search.

11. Answer: Horse
Explanation: This column lists information about a horse.

12. Answer: Hamster
Explanation: This column lists information about a hamster.

13. Answer: Giraffe
Explanation: This column lists information about a giraffe.

14. Answer: Pears, oranges, mangoes, apples, bananas
Explanation: This column lists things that grow on trees.

15. Answer: Carrots, beets, potatoes, peanuts, roots
Explanation: This column lists things that grow underground.

16. Answer: Green beans, tomatoes, grapes, pumpkins, cucumbers
Explanation: This column lists things that grow on vines.

17. Answer: Answers will vary
Explanation: Students should be able to research a topic and sort information into provided categories.

18. Answer: Answers will vary
Explanation: Students should be able to research a topic and sort information into provided categories.

19. Answer: Answers will vary
Explanation: Students should be able to research a topic and sort information into provided categories. Note the required number.

20. Answer: Answers will vary
Explanation: Students should be able to research a topic and sort information into provided categories. Note the required number.

4.4. Range of Writing

1. Answer: D
Explanation: Li should remove this sentence from the essay. It is not relevant to the main idea.

2. Answer: B
Explanation: The sentence "There are cute pandas, fuzzy foxes and ferocious mountain lions in this area" is the best revision to make this sentence more descriptive.

3. Answer: A
Explanation: A run-on sentence happens when two independent sentences are combined improperly. Sentence 3 is a run-on sentence.

4. Answer: C
Explanation: The sentence is best revised as follows: This was great because we were able to see the exhibits as the announcer told us facts about the animals. My little brother, who loves buses, enjoyed the tour.

5. Answer: B
Explanation: There should be a question mark at the end of the sentence.

6. Answer: C
Explanation: A fragment is an incomplete sentence. Sentence 5 is a fragment.

4. WRITING

prepaze

ANSWER KEY

7.   Answer: A

Explanation: The sentence "The San Diego Zoo is a fun and educational experience" is the best revision for this sentence.

8.   Answer: Answers will vary

Explanation: Students should include an introduction, body, and conclusion in their essay. The main idea and supporting details should be clear.

9.   Answer: B

Explanation: The students should use their notes to start developing an outline.

10.   Answer: A

Explanation: The sentence "The seed became a plant after 5 weeks of various changes" is the best example of the main idea for this essay.

11.   Answer: D

Explanation: The sentence "At week 3, the seed started sprouting above the ground" best supports the main idea.

12.   Answer: B

Explanation: The sentence "Finally, the seed had grown into a full plant" is the best example of a concluding statement for this report.

13.   Answer: B

Explanation: This statement is false. The students should not start writing their reports during week 1.

14.   Answer: A

Explanation: This statement is true. The students can use other resources, such as books, to write the report.

15.   Answer: A

Explanation: This statement is true. Observing and taking notes are part of the writing process.

16.   Answer: B

Explanation: This statement is false. The students can use their observation notes and other resources to write the report.

17.   Answer: B

Explanation: This statement is false. Sometimes observation reports need to be revised.

18.   Answer: Answers will vary

Explanation: Students should be able to develop an introductory paragraph with a clear main idea.

19.   Answer: Answers will vary

Explanation: Students should be able to explain how research is the first part of the writing process. In this example, the students' observations are part of the research process.

20.   Answer: Answers will vary

Explanation: Students should demonstrate an understanding of how extended writing assignments are completed over time (days, weeks, etc.). Mr. Potter's project requires that the students conduct research for a series of weeks, followed by a written report.

4.5. Chapter Review

1.   Answer: B

Explanation: This response best matches the prompt's purpose.

2.   Answer: A

Explanation: This response best matches the prompt's purpose.

3.   Answer: Answers will vary

Explanation: Students should be able to produce writing that is appropriate to the task and purpose.

4. WRITING

4. Answer: A

Explanation: A dictionary should be used to look up definitions.

5. Answer: A

Explanation: This information is best located on a map.

6. Answer: Thomas Kinkade

Explanation: The keywords needed for the search would be who or what the sentence is mostly about.

7. Answer: He has traveled all over Arizona, New Mexico, and Utah.

Explanation: "He" is the first word in the sentence, so it should be capitalized. Also, "Arizona", "New Mexico", and "Utah" are proper nouns, since they refer to specific states, so they should be capitalized. Also, since the three states are being listed, commas are required. Three states are being listed, so two commas are required.

8. Answer: I bought grapes, bread, and milk at the store.

Explanation: These three sentences can be combined by listing the three purchased items in a series and joining them with the conjunction 'and' and commas as indicated.

9. Answer: Answers will vary

Explanation: Students should be able to plan and organize ideas in the form of an outline before writing.

10. Answer: Answers will vary

Explanation: Students should be able to explain how to use technology, such as word processing programs, to produce writing.

11. Answer: D

Explanation: Sending information long best be done via email.

12. Answer: D

Explanation: Because the teacher is asking you to write about your best vacation, that means you will be writing an opinion piece.

13. Answer: B

Explanation: If you want to persuade readers to wear seatbelts, a good reason to include would be how they can prevent people who wear them from being seriously hurt.

14. Answer: D

Explanation: All of the answer choices are linking words or phrases.

15. Answer: A

Explanation: Because the teacher is asking you to write about how dolphins communicate, that means you will be writing an informative text.

16. Answer: A

Explanation: The word *who* is not a linking word.

17. Answer: B

Explanation: This statement is false. When writing an informative text, you should not include characters and dialogue.

18. Answer: A

Explanation: This statement is true. This is an example of an introductory statement.

19. Answer: B

Explanation: This statement is false. If you were writing facts about Martin Luther King, Jr., you would be writing an informative text.

20. Answer: A

Explanation: This statement is true. Narratives use dialogue and descriptions to show how characters respond to situations.

4. WRITING

prepaze

ANSWER KEY

21. Answer: A
Explanation: This statement is true. The words "before" and "first" are examples of temporal words that signal event order.

22. Answer: Answers will vary
Explanation: Students should be able to write narratives to develop real or imagined experiences or events using an effective technique.

23. Answer: Cactus, camels, scorpions, rock plants, sand
Explanation: This column lists things found in the desert.

24. Answer: Whales, salt water, jellyfish, deep sea fishing, seashells
Explanation: This column lists things found in the ocean.

25. Answer: Mountain lions, bears, squirrels, rabbits, tall trees
Explanation: This column lists things found near mountains.

26. Answer: Answers will vary
Explanation: Students should be able to explain how to gather information from sources and take brief notes.

27. Answer: C
Explanation: Joshua should start researching his topic.

28. Answer: A
Explanation: Joshua should refer to a resource, such as an American history book, before he writes his essay.

29. Answer: B
Explanation: An essay outline should include the topic, main idea, introduction, supporting details, and conclusion.

30. Answer: B
Explanation: A rough draft is the first version of an essay.

5. LANGUAGE

5.1. Conventions of Standard English

1. Answer: A
Explanation: The word "island" is a noun.

2. Answer: D
Explanation: The word "drove" is a verb.

3. Answer: B
Explanation: The word "they" is a pronoun.

4. Answer: A
Explanation: The plural form of "deer" is "deer".

5. Answer: C
Explanation: The plural form of "fox" is "foxes".

6. Answer: D
Explanation: The plural form of "ox" is "oxen".

7. Answer: B
Explanation: The student should recognize "strength" as the abstract noun because it is a noun that a person cannot see, hear, smell, touch, or taste.

8. Answer: B
Explanation: Because there is only one Katie and it is her computer, the correct choice is "Katie's".

9. Answer: B
Explanation: Because there is only one family and it is their house, the correct choice is "family's".

10. Answer: D
Explanation: Because there are multiple firefighters and the helmets belong to them, the correct choice is "firefighters'".

ANSWER KEY

11. Answer: C
Explanation: The word "sitted" is not a correctly spelled word.

12. Answer: D
Explanation: The word "smilling" is not a correctly spelled word.

13. Answer: D
Explanation: The word "crys" is not a correctly spelled word.

14. Answer: C
Explanation: The word "happyness" is not a correctly spelled word.

15. Answer: C
Explanation: The student should recognize the missing word is spelled: badge.

16. Answer: Answers will vary.
Explanation: The student should combine the two sentences into one sentence using a coordinating conjunction. Here is an example: "My homework was difficult, and it took me a long time to complete."

17. Answer: Answers will vary.
Explanation: The student should combine the two sentences into one sentence using a coordinating conjunction. Here is an example: "The frog was really slippery, so it jumped out of my hand."

18. Answer: Answers will vary.
Explanation: The student should combine the two sentences into one sentence using a subordinating conjunction. Here is an example: "I woke up scared because I had a nightmare."

19. Answer: Answers will vary.
Explanation: The student should combine the two sentences into one sentence using a subordinating conjunction. Here is an example: "Before she realized her mom was picking her up, she walked home from school."

20. Answer: I was so tired after a long day playing baseball in the hot weather. My sister whispered, "Are you asleep?" "Yes, I was," I responded in anger. "Sorry, I didn't know you were that tired," she said. The room was quiet again. I quickly fell back into a deep sleep.

Explanation: The student should understand where to place commas and quotation marks in dialogue.

5.2. Knowledge of Language

1. Answer: D
Explanation: The phrase "dizzy-looking figure eight" describes how the puppy was running.

2. Answer: A
Explanation: The word "slippery" describes the feel of the tadpole.

3. Answer: D
Explanation: The phrase "leaped like a frog" describes how the boy jumped in excitement.

4. Answer: D
Explanation: The phrase "covered in shiny diamonds" describes how the snow looked on the ground.

5. Answer: D
Explanation: The phrase "danced in the twirling wind" describes how the daisies moved in the breeze.

6. Answer: A
Explanation: The word "playful" describes the dolphins' behavior.

7. Answer: C
Explanation: The phrase "shrieking scream" describes how the boiling water sounded when it came out of the kettle.

5. LANGUAGE

ANSWER KEY

8. Answer: D

Explanation: The phrase "a bright, shiny smile that lit up her face" describes how the teacher felt about seeing her students on the first day of school.

9. Answer: C

Explanation: The phrase "quickly shoot up their pointy ears and freeze" describes how the rabbits responded when hearing Ms. Franklin tap on the window.

10. Answer: B

Explanation: The phrase "hungry for a victory" describes how the hometown team felt about winning the basketball game.

11. Answer: C

Explanation: The phrase "quickly glided above the crystal blue water" describes how the eagle caught its prey.

12. Answer: C

Explanation: The phrase "slip and slide up and down the ice rink" describes how the friends looked as they were ice skating.

13. Answer: A

Explanation: This is formal English because no slang words are used and shows respect by using the word "sir".

14. Answer: A

Explanation: This is informal English because it uses the slang word "dude".

15. Answer: B

Explanation: This is formal English, not informal English.

16. Answer: A

Explanation: This is formal English because it shows respect and courtesy by using the word "please".

17. Answer: A

Explanation: This is informal English because it uses the abbreviation "LOL!"

18. Answer: B

Explanation: This is formal English because no slang words are used. It is not informal English.

19. Answer: A

Explanation: The passage is written in formal English. It is written in complete sentences and uses the correct grammar and spelling.

20. Answer: A

Explanation: The passage is spoken in informal English. The passage is a dialogue. It uses slang words and is not written using correct grammar.

5.3. Vocabulary Acquisition and Use

1. Answer: Answers will vary

Explanation: Answers will vary but should include that the Fox means that he will say that she is a better singer than the other birds.

2. Answer: Answers will vary

Explanation: Answers will vary but should include that the author is telling us that the fox is creative and a trickster.

3. Answer: Answers will vary

Explanation: Answers will vary but should include that the fox is saying that the bird has a voice but it is not beautiful.

4. Answer: B

Explanation: The bird does not have a nice voice but it is not broken.

5. Answer: B

Explanation: The fox was using a figure of speech. She will not literally become a queen.

6. Answer: Answers will vary

Explanation: Answers will vary but should

include that the hare thinks of creative and sometimes sneaky ideas.

7.   Answer: angry
Explanation: Furious is another word for angry.

8.   Answer: C
Explanation: The mischief in the story is taking the lions food.

9.   Answer: Answers will vary
Explanation: Answers should include that this line sets the stage for rest of the poem by telling us that rest of the poem will be about what makes the author feel glad.

10.   Answer: Answers will vary
Explanation: Answers should include that this is a poem and a responsible rational such as it having stanzas or line breaks.

11.   Answer: Answers will vary
Explanation: Answers should include a responsible rational such as the author wanted a pause here for the pacing of the poem.

12.   Answer: lines
Explanation: Stanzas are made up of lines.

13.   Answer: three
Explanation: This poem has 3 stanzas.

14.   Answer: Paragraphs
Explanation: This story is broken up into paragraphs.

15.   Answer: characters
Explanation: The people in the story are the characters.

16.   Answer: C
Explanation: This writing is a story.

17.   Answer: Answers will vary
Explanation: Answers will vary but should include that this story is written in third

person and a reasonable rational such as "I know because the person telling the story is not in the story."

18.   Answer: Answers will vary
Explanation: Answers will vary but should include that the job does pay well according to the narrator.

19.   Answer: Answers will vary
Explanation: Answers will vary but should include if they agree or disagree and a reasonable explanation.

20.   Answer: Peter
Explanation: Peter felt nervous.

5. 4. Chapter Review

1.   Answer: A
Explanation: The student should understand that the phrase "I walked" is the past tense form of the verb walk. The key word "yesterday" is a clue to the reader.

2.   Answer: B
Explanation: The student should understand that the phrase "I walk" is the present tense form of the verb walk. The key words "quickly back" are a clue to the reader.

3.   Answer: C
Explanation: The student should understand that the phrase "I will walk" is the future tense form of the verb walk. The key words "next week" are a clue to the reader.

4.   Answer: B
Explanation: Churn means to turn around a circle.

5.   Answer: B
Explanation: The student should recognize the missing word is spelled: distance.

5. LANGUAGE

ANSWER KEY

6. Answer: A
Explanation: The student should recognize the missing word is spelled: balloon.

7. Answer: B
Explanation: The student should recognize the missing word is spelled: emptied.

8. Answer: C
Explanation: The phrase "quickly glided above the crystal blue water" describes how the eagle caught its prey.

9. Answer: C
Explanation: The phrase "slip and slide up and down the ice rink" describes how the friends looked as they were ice skating.

10. Answer: B
Explanation: The passage is spoken in formal English. The passage is a dialogue. It is written using correct spelling and grammar.

11 Answer: Answers will vary
Explanation: Answers will vary but should include that the phrase is describing how the cat is sitting. Roger is sitting tall and motionless, focused like a hen would be.

12 Answer: Answers will vary
Explanation: Answers will vary but should include bounded means that the cat ran/jumped forcefully.

13 Answer: Answers will vary
Explanation: Answers will vary but should include that yowl means to make loud, wailing noises or cries.

14 Answer: B
Explanation: Melissa's stomach feels like it is twisting up, it is not literally twisting up.

15 Answer: A
Explanation: The story says she stomped, which is another way to say loudly and angrily walked.

16 Answer: Answers will vary
Explanation: Answers should include that these names tell us which character says the next line.

17 Answer: Answers will vary
Explanation: Answers should include that the stage should be decorated with pictures of ponies and toy ponies as described in the stage directions at the top of the script.

18 Answer: Jane's playroom
Explanation: The stage directions tell us that they are in Jane's playroom.

19 Answer: D
Explanation: The narrator is telling this part of the story.

20 Answer: B
Explanation: The passage is written in the third person.

21 Answer: Answers will vary
Explanation: Answers will vary but should include that this story is told by a narrator and a reasonable rational such as, "I know because the story is in the third person."

22 Answer: Answers will vary
Explanation: Answers will vary but should include how they would feel if they had a rooster that laid golden eggs and how their feelings would be the same or different than the man's feelings.

23 Answer: Answers will vary
Explanation: Answers will vary but should include that the narrator thinks the man is foolish or selfish.

24 Answer: Answers will vary
Explanation: Answers will vary but should include that the man does not care about the goose, he just cares about the golden eggs and getting rich.

www.prepaze.com

ANSWER KEY

25 Answer: B
Explanation: The passage is written in third person.

26 Answer: setting
Explanation: The setting is where a story takes place.

27 Answer: script
Explanation: Plays are written as scripts.

28 Answer: scenes
Explanation: Acts are made up of scenes.

29 Answer: Answers will vary
Explanation: Answers will vary but should include that the boy was waving his hand motioning for Amra to come over to them.

30 Answer: Answers will vary
Explanation: Answers will vary but should include that a gaggle means a loud or rowdy group of people.

END OF YEAR ASSESSMENT

1. Answer: B
Explanation: Based on context clues from the text, the emperor is best described as proud and greedy. The text states that he spends too much money on clothes.

2. Answer: D
Explanation: The weavers did not make clothes for the emperor because they were not real weavers.

3. Answer: A
Explanation: This statement is true. When writing a narrative, you should describe the thoughts and feelings of the characters.

4. Answer: Answers will vary
Explanation: Students should be able to write narratives to develop real or imagined experiences or events using an effective technique.

5. Answer: C
Explanation: Jamestown is in the green area on the map. This shows it is a southern colony.

6. Answer: D
Explanation: The men were not looking for a buried treasure.

7. Answer: C
Explanation: The internet is the best program for researching this information.

8. Answer: University of North Carolina
Explanation: Michael Jordan's basketball career began as a player for the University of North Carolina.

9. Answer: Three
Explanation: Michael Jordan quit playing basketball a total of three times throughout his career.

10. Answer: Answers will vary
Explanation: Students should be able to produce writing that is appropriate to the task and purpose.

11. Answer: B

Explanation: The story's mood is best described as dark and somber.

12. Answer: D
Explanation: All of these sentences demonstrate the mood of the story.

13. Answer: Answers will vary
Explanation: Students should demonstrate an awareness that the central message of a story is a lesson or moral that the author wants to convey.

prepaze

ANSWER KEY

14. **Answer: Answers will vary**
Explanation: Students should demonstrate an awareness of how a story's central message can be conveyed through the characters' experience. The central message of this story is about being gentle rather than forceful.

15. **Answer: A**
Explanation: The text near number 1 contains information about spiders in homes.

16. **Answer: B**
Explanation: The text near number 3 contains information about how much spiders eat.

17. **Answer: Answers will vary**
Explanation: Students should be able to write an informative text and develop the topic with facts, definitions, and details.

18. **Answer: A**
Explanation: The word *thrive* most likely means to live and grow in the context of this text.

19. **Answer: D**
Explanation: The word *beneficial* most likely means helpful in the context of this text.

20. **Answer: Food chain**
Explanation: Both passages explain how plants and humans are part of the food chain.

21. **Answer: plant**
Explanation: Passage 2, offers more details about the plant's role in the food chain than passage 2.

22. **Answer: B**
Explanation: The narrator is the child of the father in the story.

While the age and gender of the narrator is not clear, he or she uses the phrase "my father" in reference to the main character.

23. **Answer: D**
Explanation: This story is told from the third person omniscient point-of-view. The narrator knows the thoughts and actions of all characters in the story.

24. **Answer: Answers will vary**
Explanation: Students should be able to write an opinion piece about the story and distinguish their own point of view from that of the narrator/characters.

25. **Answer: D**
Explanation: This article discusses limiting the use of digital devices for children.

26. **Answer: B**
Explanation: The author position is that parents should set rules when allowing their children to use digital devices.

27. **Answer: Answers will vary**
Explanation: Students should be able to write an opinion piece about a specific topic.

28. **Answer: Answers will vary**
Explanation: The word *extraordinary* means *unusual*. Some other possible answers include *different, special* or *amazing*.

29. **Answer: Answers will vary**
Explanation: The word *gracefully* means *delicately*. Some other possible answers include *smoothly*.

ANSWER KEY

30.   Answer: Answers will vary
Explanation: Students should be able to answer questions by referring explicitly to the text. The text states that the heart has important body functions such as pumping blood to every part of the body.|

31.   Answer: A
Explanation: This statement is true. Both stories create imagery about the weather.

32.   Answer: B
Explanation: This statement is false. These stories do not feature the same characters in a different setting.

33.   Answer: A
Explanation: The main idea of this text is that batteries are important because they power portable devices.

34.   Answer: C
Explanation: The following sentence best demonstrates cause and effect: Without batteries, many of the devices we use while on the go would not work.

35.   Answer: scenes
Explanation: The play is divided into parts called scenes.

36.   Answer: act
Explanation: The scenes are part of an act.

37.   Answer: Answers will vary
Explanation: Students should be able to list at least five characters in the play: the witches, Duncan, Captain, Malcolm, Donalbain, and Lennox.

38.   Answer: B
Explanation: The text states that by 1907, about two million Americans had visited a nickelodeon. This event happened before the other answer choices.

39.   Answer: A
Explanation: New technology allowed movie theaters to play longer films.

40.   Answer: Did you bring the note, the pen, and the watch?
Explanation: These three questions can be combined into a single question by combining the objects into a series and joining them with the conjunction 'and'. Commas are required as indicated.

41.   Answer: Answers will vary
Explanation: Students should be able to plan and organize ideas in the form of an outline before writing.

42.   Answer: C
Explanation: The encyclopedia would be the best way to look up this information.

43.   Answer: C
Explanation: Joshua should make revisions to his rough draft on Day 4.

44.   Answer: D
Explanation: All of these ideas would be helpful for making revisions to an essay.

45.   Answer: Answers will vary
Explanation: Students should be able to research a topic and sort information into provided categories.

END OF YEAR ASSESSMENT

Copyrighted Material   prepaze

REFERENCES CITED

- *Anansi and the Pot of Beans (A West African Folktale),* Retold by Amy Friedman and Meredith Johnson

- *Excerpt from Call it Courage,* By Armstrong Perry

- *Excerpt from Daisy Dawson is on Her Way,* By Steve Voake

- *Excerpt from Fantastic Mr. Fox,* By Roald Dahl

- *Excerpt from Macbeth,* By William Shakespeare adapted by Farrar Williams

- *Excerpt from MacDonald Hall Goes Hollywood,* By Gordon Korman

- *Excerpt from Sarah Plain and Tall,* By Patricia MacLachlan

- *Excerpt from the article "Spacecraft InSight's Mission is to Find Clues on How Mars First Formed",* By Washington Post

- *Excerpt from the article "The Voice Missing from the Elephant Trophy Debate? Africans.",* By Rosie Cooney

- *Excerpt from the article "Weight Watchers Should Not be Offering its Services to Kids",* By Rebecca Scritchfield

- *Excerpt from the article Allow Kids Less Time on Digital Devices,* By Naomi Schaefer Riley

- *Excerpt from the article Eyes in the Sky,* By Jeffrey Kluger

- *Excerpt from the article Reuse, Reduce, Recycle,* From the National Institute of Environmental Health Services

- *Excerpt from the article Your Eyes,* By Kids Health

- *Excerpt from The Box-Car Children,* By Gertrude Chandler Warner

- *Excerpt from The Rainbow Fish,* By Marcus Pfister

- *Excerpt from The True Story of the Three Little Pigs,* By Jon Scieszka

- *James and the Giant Peach,* By Roald Dahl

www.prepaze.com

REFERENCES CITED

- *Julian, Secret Agent,* By Ann Cameron

- *More Stories Julian Tells,* By Ann Cameron

- *Passages* from Nationalgeographic.com

- *Spiders* from Washingtonpost.com

- *Stars and Stripes Forever,* By John Philip Sousa

- *The Ant and the Grasshopper,* From Aesop's Fables

- *The Fox and the Stork,* From Aesop's Fables

- *This Can't Be Happening at Macdonald Hall!,* By Gordon Korman

prepaze

Made in the USA
Las Vegas, NV
03 September 2021